OECD Reviews on Local Job Creation

Employment and Skills Strategies in Saskatchewan and the Yukon, Canada

OECD
BETTER POLICIES FOR BETTER LIVES

LEED
BUILDING MORE & BETTER JOBS

Please cite this publication as:
OECD (2016), *Employment and Skills Strategies in Saskatchewan and the Yukon, Canada*, OECD Reviews on Local Job Creation, OECD Publishing, Paris.
http://dx.doi.org/10.1787/9789264259225-en

ISBN 978-92-64-25920-1 (print)
ISBN 978-92-64-25921-8 (PDF)
ISBN 978-92-64-25922-5 (e-pub)

Series: OECD Reviews on Local Job Creation
ISSN 2311-2328 (print)
ISSN 2311-2336 (online)

Photo credits: © Andy Dean Photography/Shutterstock.com; © Sai Tha/Shutterstock.com

Corrigenda to OECD publications may be found on line at: *www.oecd.org/publishing/corrigenda*.

Foreword

This review has been written by the Local Economic and Employment Development (LEED) Programme of the Organisation for Economic Co-operation and Development (OECD) as part of a project undertaken in co-operation with Employment and Social Development Canada, the Ontario Ministry of Training, Colleges, and Universities and the Saskatchewan Ministry of the Economy and Yukon's Department of Education. This project is part of the OECD LEED programme of work under the leadership of Sylvain Giguère, Head of Division, who reviewed this report.

The principal authors are Thomas Townsend (University of Ottawa) and Jonathan Barr (OECD). Michela Meghnagi and Pierre Georgin provided valuable statistical and data analysis support, which was critical to the production of this report. Thanks also go to François Iglesias for production assistance and Janine Treves who provided useful editorial support.

Special thanks should be given to federal and provincial officials who contributed to this report and participated in the OECD study visits: Ramona McDowell and Saloie Moreno, Employment and Social Development Canada; Leah Goodwin, Ministry of the Economy, Saskatchewan; and Judy Thrower, Anton Solomon, and Shawn Kitchen, the Yukon Department of Education.

Special thanks should also be given to local stakeholders and indigenous groups in each of the case study areas, who participated in meetings and provided documentation and comments critical to the production of the report.

Table of contents

Tables

Figures

Acronyms and abbreviations

ASETS	Aboriginal Skills Employment and Training Strategy
CAF	Canada Apprenticeship Forum
CAFN	Chapagne and Aishik First Nation
CanNor	Canadian Northern Economic Development Agency
CCDA	Canada Council of Directors of Apprenticeship
CIC	Citizenship and Immigration Canada
CFP	Community Futures Program
CJFA	Canada Job Fund Agreements
CSJ	Canada Summer Jobs
CSL	Canada Student Loans
CST	Canada Social Transfer
CYFN	Council of Yukon First Nations
EI	Employment Insurance
ESDC	Employment and Social Development Canada
FCR	Foreign Credential Recognition
FCRP	Foreign Credential Recognition Program
FLMM	Forum of Labour Market Ministers
FNGPA	First Nations Governance and Public Administration
FNLT	First Nations Leadership Training
INAC	Indigenous and Northern Affairs Canada
LEED	Local Economic and Employment Development
LMDA	Labour Market Development Agreement
LMI	Labour Market Information
NAFC	National Association of Friendship Centres
NEET	Not in Employment, Education or Training
NSERC	Natural Sciences and Engineering Research Council of Canada
OECD	Organisation for Economic Co-operation and Development
PBO	Parliamentary Budget Office
SGS	Self-Governing Secretariat
SGYFN	Self Governing Yukon First Nations
TIOW	Targeted Initiative for Older Workers
WD	Western Economic Diversification Canada
WS	Work Sharing
YES	Youth Employment Strategy
YBS	Yukon Bureau of Statistics

Executive summary

While Canada has experienced a fairly solid labour market recovery, prospects for growth remain cloudy due to volatility from low oil prices and increasing household debt. Demographic pressures require productivity improvements in the economy and a need to make better use of the existing skills of the workforce. Employment and skills policies are critical levers in boosting economic development opportunities but effective implementation requires strong capacity at the local level.

The OECD Local Economic and Employment Development (LEED) programme has developed its reviews on Local Job Creation as an international cross-comparative study to examine the contributions of local labour market policy to boosting quality employment and productivity. To help Canada respond to current and future labour market challenges, this review has looked at a range of institutions and bodies involved in employment and skills development policies. In addition to reviewing the national policy framework, in-depth work was undertaken across four local areas within two jurisdictions in Canada to understand local implementation capacities and opportunities: the Yukon and Saskatchewan.

Indigenous Peoples in Canada face a number of significant employment and economic development challenges. Unemployment for Indigenous Peoples in Canada was 12.4% in 2015, which is double the rate of the non-indigenous population of 6.8%. The Canadian Government has signalled its intention to "renew" its relationship with its Indigenous Peoples. A key focus of this OECD review was on emerging employment and economic development opportunities for indigenous communities. Self-government agreements are changing the face of indigenous governance and altering the relationship between these communities and the federal government.

Yukon's labour market activities are driven from the conclusion of a Labour Market Framework agreement, which includes a far-reaching series of stakeholder committees covering skills and training; immigration; labour market information; and recruitment and employee retention. This agreement provides the basis to stimulate robust networks at the local level and establish stronger mechanisms to increase the voice of employers in skills development opportunities. In Saskatchewan, the Plan for Growth has been effective in focusing and coordinating the efforts of various Ministries by providing an integrated approach and promoting better cross ministry policy co-ordination. However, more needs to be done to integrate service arrangements at the local level in cities such as Regina for the benefit for job seekers and employers.

Over 30% of Canada's Indigenous Peoples live in either Saskatchewan or the Yukon. Overall, the OECD review found that the Yukon and Saskatchewan have demonstrated leadership in establishing stronger "government to government" relationships with indigenous communities. Strong efforts are being made in both regions to improve access to employment and skills development opportunities through a number of innovative programmes. Going forward, sustained efforts must be placed on providing indigenous communities with job opportunities that will contribute to their overall economic and social well-being. Building the leadership and governance capacities of indigenous communities should be a priority. The following key conclusions and recommendations are intended to help build and expand on the recent and ongoing reforms in Canada.

Key conclusions and recommendations

Recommendations for boosting local employment and economic development opportunities of indigenous communities

- Recognise that provincial and territorial governments are playing an increasingly active role in indigenous communities and have considerable incentives to ensure successful economic and social development. This may well involve rethinking the federal leadership role in areas where provinces and territories have strong capacity and competence.
- Strategically use public procurement policies to add conditions on contracts around the employment of indigenous individuals and/or to increase the number of apprenticeship and training opportunities.
- Strengthen leadership capacities and facilitate information sharing to enable identification of the most promising conditions for success across Canada's indigenous communities by establishing a repository of effective practices in promoting indigenous employment and skills development activities.

Towards an action plan for jobs: Recommendations for Saskatchewan

- Promote stronger local employment and economic development networks and inject greater flexibility into the management and implementation of policies at the local level.
- Encourage labour market development stakeholders – including colleges and universities – to become more engaged in accessing, analyzing, and producing local labour market information. This includes developing stronger forecasting methods of future skill needs as well as informing students of potential job opportunities.
- Expand the use of demand driven training through stronger linkages with local employers (especially SMEs) and embed skills policies in economic development thinking.
- Implement a comprehensive provincial youth employment strategy which focuses on employment and job creation as well as smoother transitions into the labour market.

Towards an action plan for jobs: Recommendations for Yukon

- Build on the success of the Labour Market Framework by establishing local networks in communities in the Yukon that would be tasked with developing employment and economic development plans. These networks should involve employers and be closely connected to the training system.
- Place policy priority on increasing the engagement of employers with the vocational education system to ensure they are providing advice on the relevancy of programmes and curriculum.
- Develop an entrepreneurship strategy, which focuses on youth and older workers and Indigenous Peoples as a tool for economic adjustment and job creation.

- Develop a youth employment strategy focusing on pathways to success with the goal of reducing early school leaving, increasing participation in postsecondary education and connecting low-skilled youth to the labour market.
- Establish a balance between employers needs for workers and job seekers needs for entry-level opportunities by instituting a requirement for a labour market assessment as part of the process of determining what skills will be sought through the Provincial Nominee Program.

Reader's guide

The *Local Job Creation* project involves a series of country reviews in Australia, Belgium (Flanders), Canada (Ontario, Quebec, Saskatchewan, and the Yukon), Czech Republic, France, Ireland, Israel, Italy (Autonomous Province of Trento), Korea, Poland, Slovenia, Sweden, Turkey, the United Kingdom and the United States (California and Michigan). The key stages of each review are summarised in Box 1.

Box 1. **Summary of the OECD LEED Local Job Creation Project Methodology**

- Analyse available data to understand the key labour market challenges facing the country in the context of the economic recovery and apply an OECD LEED diagnostic tool which seeks to assess the balance between the supply and demand for skills at the local level.
- Map the current policy framework for local job creation in the country.
- Apply the local job creation dashboard, developed by the OECD LEED Programme (Froy et al., 2010) to measure the relative strengths and weaknesses of local employment and training agencies to contribute to job creation.
- Conduct an OECD study visit, where local and national roundtables with a diverse range of stakeholders are held to discuss the results and refine the findings and recommendations.
- Contribute to policy development in the reviewed country by proposing policy options to overcome barriers, illustrated by selected good practice initiatives from other OECD countries.

While the project was conceived at a time when the economic crisis was the primary focus of policy makers, it was clear that both short-term and longer-term actions would be needed to ensure sustainable economic growth. In response to this issue, the OECD LEED Programme has developed a set of thematic areas on which local stakeholders and employment and training agencies can focus to build employment growth at the local level. These include:

1. **Better aligning policies and programmes to local economic development challenges and opportunities;**
2. **Adding value through skills:** Creating an adaptable skilled labour force and supporting employment progression and skills upgrading;
3. **Targeting policy to local employment sectors and investing in quality jobs**, including gearing education and training to emerging local growth sectors and responding to global trends, while working with employers on skills utilisation and productivity; and,
4. **Being inclusive** to ensure that all actual and potential members of the labour force can contribute to future economic growth.

Local Job Creation Dashboard

As part of the project, the OECD LEED Programme has drawn on its previous research to develop a set of best practice priorities, which is used to assess local practices through a local job creation dashboard (see Box 2). The dashboard enables national and local policy-makers to gain a stronger overview of the strengths and weaknesses of the current policy framework, whilst better prioritising future actions and resources. A value between 1 (low) to 5 (high) is assigned to each of the four priority areas corresponding to the relative strengths and weaknesses of local policy approaches based on best practices in other OECD countries.

Box 2. **Local Job Creation Dashboard**

Better aligning policies and programmes to local economic development

1.1. Flexibility in the delivery of employment and vocational training policies

1.2. Capacities within employment and VET sectors

1.3. Policy co-ordination, policy integration and co-operation with other sectors

1.4. Evidence based policy making

Adding value through skills

2.1. Flexible training open to all in a broad range of sectors

2.2. Working with employers on training

2.3. Matching people to jobs and facilitating progression

2.4. Joined up approaches to skills

Targeting policy to local employment sectors and investing in quality jobs

3.1. Relevance of provision to important local employment sectors and global trends and challenges

3.2. Working with employers on skills utilisation and productivity

3.3. Promotion of skills for entrepreneurship

3.4. Promoting quality jobs through local economic development

Being inclusive

4.1. Employment and training programmes geared to local "at-risk" groups

4.2. Childcare and family friendly policies to support women's participation in employment

4.3. Tackling youth unemployment

4.4. Openness to immigration

The approach for Canada

This study has looked at the range of institutions and bodies involved in workforce, skills, and economic development in Canada. A first study was completed and published in 2014 focusing on Ontario and Quebec. For this second review, in-depth field work was undertaken across four case study areas in two jurisdictions: the province of Saskatchewan and Yukon (one of three territories in Canada). Compared to Ontario and Quebec, these jurisdictions are smaller in size; Saskatchewan has a population of 1.2 million people and Yukon's population is 36 000. The four case study areas – representing two in each jurisdiction are:

Saskatchewan

- Regina (the provincial capital).
- Whitecap (the territory of the Whitecap Dakota First Nation).

Yukon

- Whitehorse (the territorial capital).
- Dawson City (a small community 500 kms north of Whitehorse).

In each, a country expert conducted interviews with a range of local stakeholders, including employment offices, economic development officials, training institutions, employers, and other local community and social inclusion organisations. Additionally, local roundtables and a meeting with provincial and territorial level officials were held in each case study location in September 2015 to discuss the findings and recommendations.

The next section of the report provides an overview of key economic and labour market trends in Canada. The subsequent chapters provide an overview of the key economic trends in Saskatchewan and the Yukon. This is followed by the results of the study in Saskatchewan and Yukon in the form of a local job creation dashboard. This section of the report highlights strengths and weaknesses of local policy approaches and actions taken in each jurisdiction. Drawing on these findings, the final section of the report provides recommendations for consideration for Saskatchewan, the Yukon, and the federal government in the development of an action plan, which will contribute to quality job creation at the local level.

Chapter 1

Policy context for employment and skills in Canada

Among OECD countries, Canada's economy weathered the economic crisis relatively well but has faced recent uncertainty as a result of volatility in oil prices. While Canada has a solid foundation of skills upon which to build future growth, demographic pressures will require the country to make better use of the skills of the existing workforce to enhance productivity. This chapter provides an overview of key economic and employment trends in Canada, including a focus on key labour market challenges facing Indigenous Peoples.

Key economic and labour market trends in Canada

Economic trends

Canada experienced a milder recession and a quicker recovery than most OECD member countries. As shown in Figure 1.1, while GDP shrank in 2009, positive growth resumed in 2010 and Canada had been consistently performing better than the OECD average until 2014. In the first half of 2015, Canada experienced a technical recession and, while turning positive in the second half of 2015, Canada's GDP growth was estimated to be between 1-1.5%. According to OECD projections, after two years of below average performance in 2015 and 2016, GDP growth in Canada will be in line with the average of OECD countries in 2017.

Figure 1.1. **Annual real GDP growth in Canada and the OECD, 2007-17**

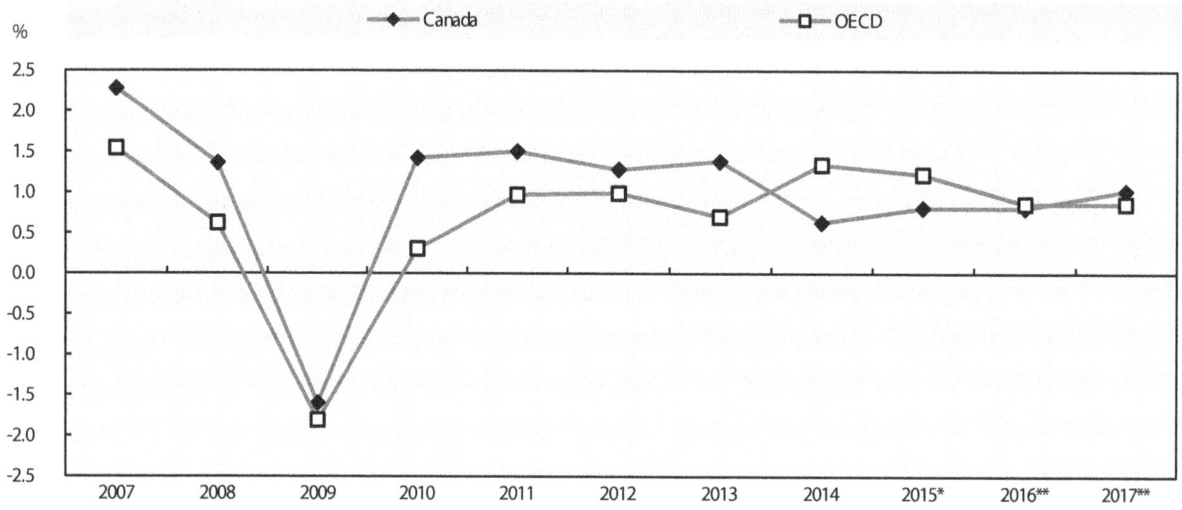

* OECD projections for OECD average, actual data for Canada.
** OECD projections for OECD average and Canada.
Source: OECD (2015a), "OECD Economic Outlook No. 98 (Edition 2015/2)", *OECD Economic Outlook: Statistics and Projections* (database), *http://dx.doi.org/10.1787/data-00688-en*.

In recent years, the significant drop in oil prices has led to a weaker Canadian dollar and reduced economic activity in regions that are linked to the energy sector, notably Alberta, Newfoundland and Labrador and Saskatchewan (RBC, 2014). Alberta and Newfoundland and Labrador have been hit particularly hard by this shock, however Saskatchewan has been able to weather it better thanks to its more diversified economy. In the rest of the country, lower oil prices are benefiting non-oil related exports, in particular manufacturing, and consumer spending through lower fuel costs.

According to 2014 data, the level of labour productivity in Canada, measured as GDP per hour worked, is higher than the OECD average but significantly lower than in the United States (Figure 1.2). The rate of increase in labour productivity in Canada over the last ten

Figure 1.2. **GDP per hour worked (2010 USD, constant prices)**

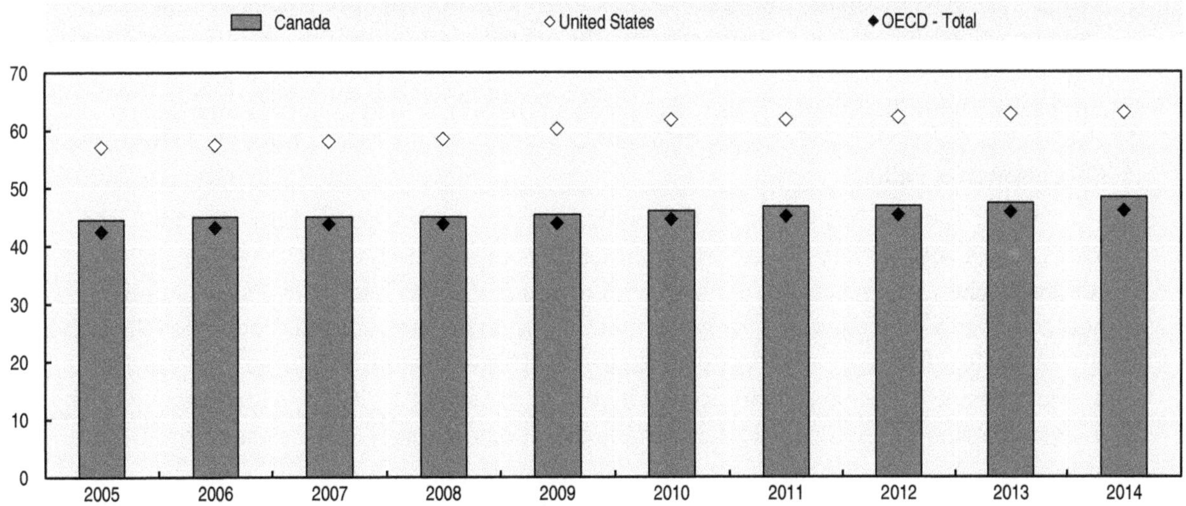

Source: OECD (2015c), "Multifactor productivity" (indicator), *http://dx.doi.org/10.1787/a40c5025-en.*

years has been similar to the OECD average (average annual growth rate of 0.9%) but slightly lower than in the United States (+1.1%).

Shortfalls in multifactor productivity (MFP), which reflects the overall efficiency of the production process, is the main cause of weak labour productivity growth in Canada (OECD, 2014). While in the United States gains in MFP have been much higher in the current recovery than in previous cycles, this has not been the case in Canada. Given the strong link between living standards and MFP growth, raising the level of MFP growth is a crucial long-term challenge for Canada. In order to address this issue, recommendations have been made by the OECD, especially in terms of improvements in tertiary education and better innovation outcomes (OECD, 2014).

Population trends

Between 2004-14, the Canadian population grew at an annual average rate of 1.1%, which is higher than the OECD average of 0.7%, and the highest rate among G7 countries (OECD, 2016; Statistics Canada, 2015a). At the sub-national level, above average population growth over the same period was observed in Nunavut (+1.9%) and in the Western provinces and territories, notably Alberta (+2.4%), Yukon (+1.6%) and Saskatchewan (+1.2%).

The annual population growth rate in Canada for the years 2014-15 is estimated to be 0.9% (Statistics Canada, 2015a), the lowest figure recorded in the last 15 years. This slowdown of demographic growth could be attributed to a decrease in the number of international immigrants arriving in the country (239 800 in 2014-15 vs 267 900 in 2013-14). For the first time since 1997, the number of non-permanent residents in Canada declined in 2014-15 (-10 300), notably due to the important fall observed in Alberta (-21 200) but also in Saskatchewan (-2 200), New Brunswick (-200) and the territories (-100).

As in many other OECD countries, the population of Canada is ageing. The population aged 65 years and older, which accounted for 16.1% of the total population in 2015, has been increasing almost three times faster than the whole population (+2.8% annual average growth rate between 2000-15, vs 1.0% for the whole population). In 2015, for the first time the elderly population (65 years or more) exceeds the number of people aged less than 14. Recent projections predict that the proportion of persons aged 65 years or older will continue to increase and reach around 20% of the population in 2024 (Statistics Canada, 2015b). All parts of Canada are not affected by this demographic trend in a similar way, with the territories and Prairie Provinces experiencing slower population ageing in comparison with the Atlantic Provinces as well as Ontario, British Columbia and Quebec.

Education and skills

Overall, Canada has a high level of skills with the largest proportion of individuals aged 25 to 64 with tertiary education among OECD countries (54% vs OECD average of 34%). However, when looking at the highest levels of education attained, only 9% of Canadians hold a master's or doctoral degree compared to 12% on average in OECD countries (OECD, 2015b). While on average, 13.7% of people aged 15-19 years in the OECD were not enrolled in education in 2014, this proportion was higher in Canada at 16.1%. This includes 7.1% of individuals who are not in education, employment or training (NEET), close to the OECD average of 7.2%.

Based on an analysis of earnings premiums for various levels of education, the OECD found that, in Canada as a whole, skills shortages at the postsecondary education level have remained stable in recent years (OECD, 2014). However, when looking at provincial data, significant increases in real earnings at all education levels revealed the presence of labour shortages in resource-rich provinces such as Alberta and Saskatchewan, with potential negative impacts on economic activity.

Labour market trends

The Canadian labour market has recovered solidly since the trough of the global economic crisis. As Figure 1.3 shows, annual employment growth was relatively high between 2010-13 compared with the OECD average, but became weaker in 2014 and is expected to remain under 1% annually until 2017.

Figure 1.3. **Annual employment growth rate, Canada and OECD average, 2007-17**

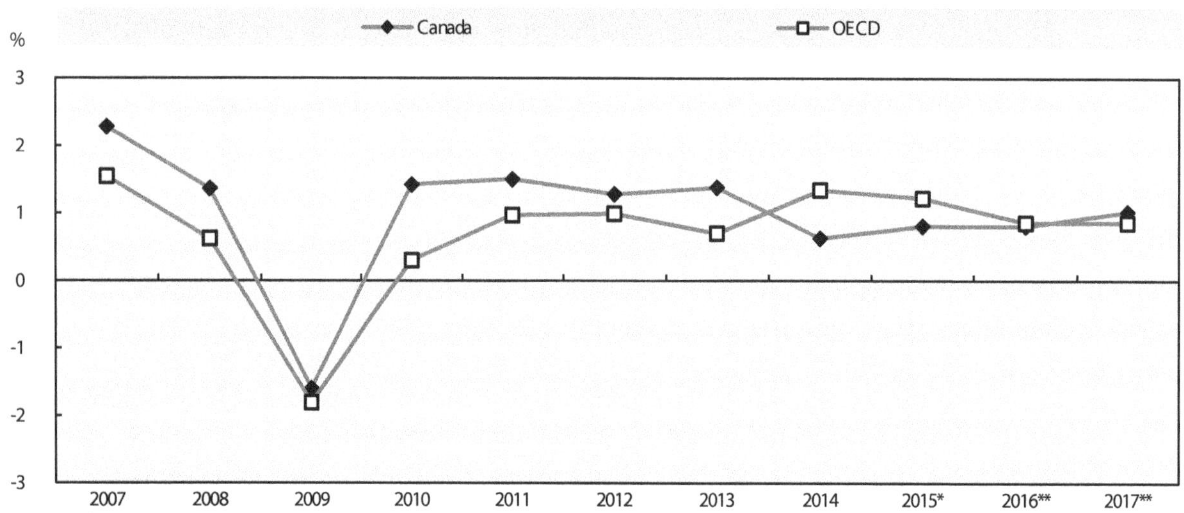

* OECD projections for OECD average, actual data for Canada.

** OECD projections for OECD average and Canada.

Source: OECD (2015a), "OECD Economic Outlook No. 98 (Edition 2015/2)", *OECD Economic Outlook: Statistics and Projections* (database), *http://dx.doi.org/10.1787/bd810434-en*.

The unemployment rate has been consistently lower than the OECD average since 2010, reaching 6.9% in 2014 (OECD average of 7.6%). The youth unemployment rate (individuals aged 15-24 years old) was lower than the average of OECD countries (13.2% vs 15.1% in 2015). And with only 13.4% of unemployed people who had been searching for a job for more than one year in the last quarter of 2014, Canada had one of the lowest rates of long-term unemployment within the OECD (OECD, 2014).

At the provincial/territorial level, large differences can be observed in terms of both the unemployment rate (Figure 1.4) and employment rate (Figure 1.5). In 2015, Yukon had

Figure 1.4. **Unemployment rate, Canadian provinces and territories,* 2015**

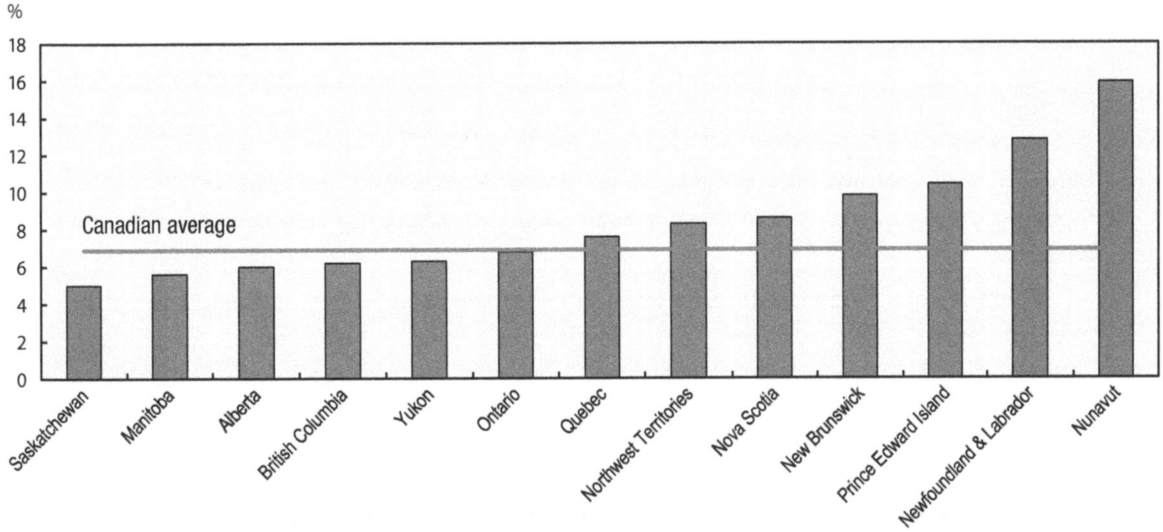

* LFS data are collected using a different methodology in the territories and in the provinces. Figures only include the off-reserve population.
** Canadian average does not include the territories.
Source: Statistics Canada. Table 282-0123 – Labour force survey estimates (LFS).

Figure 1.5. **Employment rate, Canadian provinces and territories,* 2015**

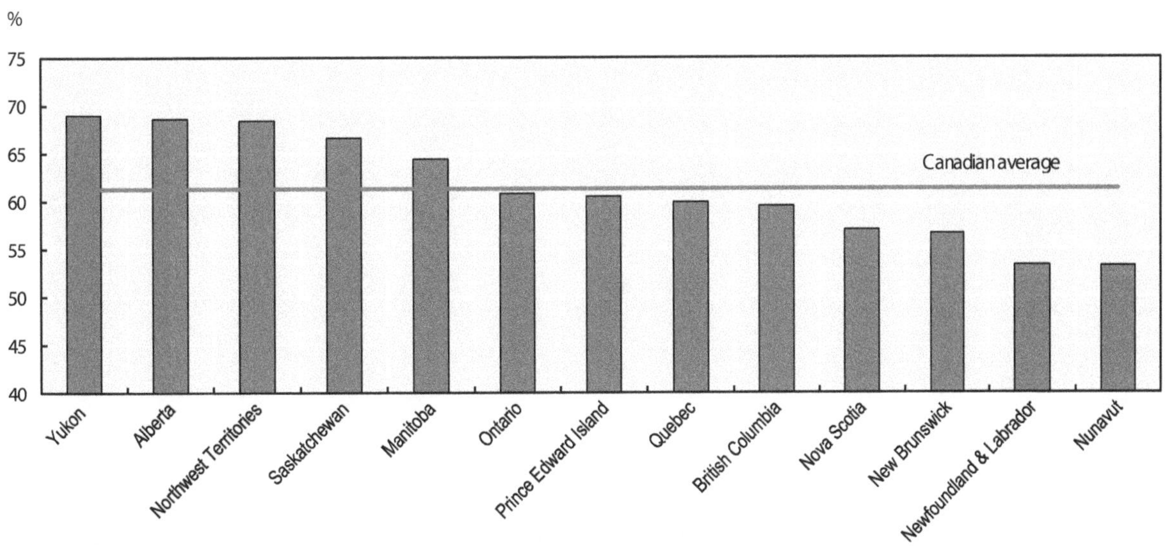

* LFS data are collected using a different methodology in the territories and in the provinces. Figures only include the off-reserve population.
** Canadian average does not include the territories.
Source: Statistics Canada. Table 282-0123 – Labour force survey estimates (LFS).

the second lowest unemployment rate (4.3%) and the highest employment rate (71.5%), while Saskatchewan recorded the lowest unemployment rate (3.8%), and an above average employment rate (67%).

Youth unemployment

In Canada, youth unemployment ("youth" being defined as the population aged 15-24) rose quickly during the contraction but has remained high, accentuating the gap between the youth and adult rates. Historically, youth unemployment rates have been about twice that for the adult population. In some regions that ratio has remained higher. Equally, youth unemployment rates for indigenous people remain substantially higher at 18.8% in 2015, compared to a non-indigenous rate of 13%.

Young people who are looking for work have little by way of financial support and in most cases only basic counselling and job search services. For those youth who fall into the NEET category, prospects are significantly lower than their better-educated counterparts. A concern with slow job growth over the last several years is the possibility of longer-term effects for new entrants into the labour market of a protracted period of insecurity before securing permanent work and downstream effects on consumer behaviour and family formation.

There is considerable debate in Canada about the scale of issues related to youth unemployment (Adele and Delic, 2014; Bernard, 2013 and 2015; Cross, 2015). The gap between the 15-24 rate versus the over 25 rate has been increasing since the early 1990's and was at 2.4 times in 2012. Additionally, youth labour market participation rates have been declining. While one explanation can be that young people are staying in school;

Figure 1.6. **Long-term unemployment rates of 15-24 year olds versus 25-54 year olds, Canada**

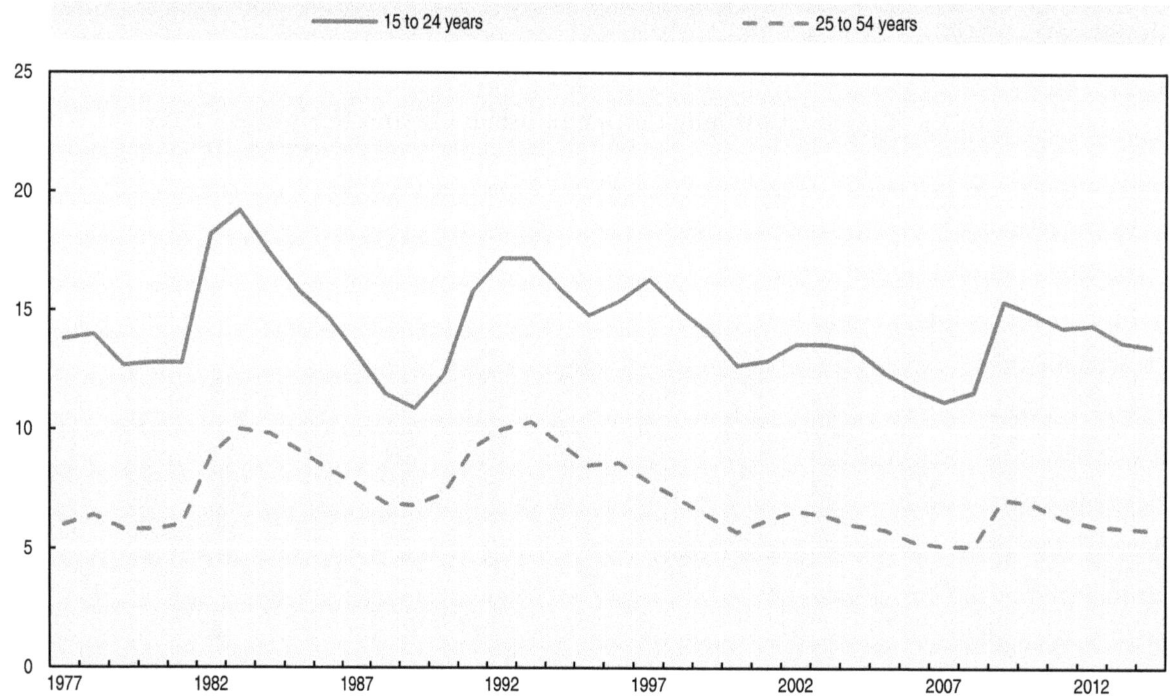

Note: Figures only include the off-reserve population.
Source: Statistics Canada, CANSIM Table 282-0002,

another could be that those youth who are in the labour force are less competitive and having a harder time securing employment. A further argument is that the data is somewhat distorted with the inclusion of 15 year olds in the calculation. Excluding 15-year-olds would reduce overall unemployment estimates by a full percentage point in most recent years. However, there is little disagreement that today's young people require better skills to secure a future in Canada's labour market and that young people without those skills occupy a precarious place in the job market.

While the duration of youth unemployment appears to be shorter (e.g. youth find jobs more quickly than their adult counterparts), they are of course less likely to be in receipt of Employment Insurance (EI) benefits and may need to take jobs that are less attractive. There are considerable variances regionally in Canada and one feature of Saskatchewan and Yukon that complicates analysis is the relatively large youth indigenous population living on-reserve, which is not accounted for in most surveys.

Current and projected labour market matching

According to the recent Job Vacancy and Wage Survey (Statistics Canada, 2015d), 400 000 job vacancies were available in Canada in the first quarter of 2015, with Ontario (153 000) and Alberta (74 000) recording the highest number of vacancies. The job vacancy rate, which corresponds to the number of job vacancies or vacant positions as a percentage of labour demand (sum of occupied positions and vacant positions), was 2.6% in Canada. Higher job vacancy rates were generally observed in the provinces and territories of Western Canada, such as Yukon (3.9%) and Alberta (3.5%), than in Central and Eastern Canada.

The highest number of job vacancies was in service support and other service occupations (42 000), which includes occupations such as specialised cleaners, food counter attendants or operators in amusement, recreation and sport. Service representatives and other customer and personal services occupations came second with 31 000 vacancies. Concerning trades related occupational groups, industrial, electrical and construction trades (17 000), and maintenance and equipment operation trades (12 000) had the largest number of job vacancies.

Although the majority of job vacancies were for full-time work (72%) in the first quarter of 2015, this was the case for only 45% of health occupations and 54% of service occupations, compared with 96% for management occupations and 95% for natural and applied sciences occupations.

Differences in the length of job vacancy durations indicate that employers are finding it more difficult to fill job vacancies in some broad sectors such as health and in specific occupations such as trades, transport and equipment operator. Conversely, jobs vacancies in occupations such business, finance and administration or art, culture, recreation and sport are easier to fill.

A recent report by Employment and Social Development Canada found no evidence of labour market imbalances in terms of broad skills levels in recent years (ESDC, 2013a). This report predicts that, over the period 2013-22, the number of job openings will be matched by similar numbers of job seekers for each broad skill level. Two-thirds of the 5.8 million job openings expected for the period 2013-22 will be in occupations requiring tertiary education or in management occupations. On the other hand, one third of job openings are projected to be in occupations requiring only on-the-job training or high school education. Almost all occupations that are expected to face labour shortages are high-skilled occupations. These include trades, transport and equipment, health, management as well as occupations in the primary sector. It can be noted that, with the exception of health, these occupations are mostly male populated. Conversely, a number of low-skilled occupations are projected to display labour surpluses, including occupations related to administrative and clerical work, and also some occupations specific to the primary and manufacturing and utilities sectors. Given the great variety of economic and industrial structures across Canadian provinces and territories, this broad analysis at the federal level may mask significant regional differences in terms of labour shortages and surpluses.

Since January 2011, Statistics Canada has conducted a monthly Job Vacancy Survey that establishes the demand for labour by employers. For the first quarter of 2015, the Yukon had the highest job vacancy rate in the country at 3.9% while Saskatchewan ranked fifth at 3.0% both above the federal average of 2.6%. One noticeable association with tight labour markets is an increase in labour force participation of older workers in those areas. In Saskatchewan for example the participation rate is 44.1% for workers over 55 years of age as opposed to 36.1% for the rest of the country. In the Yukon, the 55+ participation rate is even higher at 50%.

Job vacancies appear to be occurring in specific technical/professional areas such as nursing that will take time to remedy with sufficient workforce entrants possessing the skills required. Many of the 10 occupations with the highest number of job vacancies, however, are entry-level positions or lower skilled jobs. In some cases these reflect discrepancies between the wages on offer and the cost of living in the community. In these cases there can be simultaneously unemployed and vacant positions. An approach that has been used to fill at least some of these vacancies in the hospitality and retail sectors has been the use of nominee programmes where the province or territory can identify the skills that are in demand and recruit those skills internationally.

Another dimension of tighter labour markets is strangely a reduction in internal mobility within organisations as the result of a restructuring of the career process itself and a decline in being able to translate "learning on and through the job" into more senior positions. Employers are looking for ready to work candidates rather than favouring development and successive promotion of internal candidates. The Metcalf Foundation looked at the development of job growth over a 15 year period in Ontario and found that the growth rate of jobs requiring a university degree or college diploma was 50% while the growth rate for entry level jobs requiring lower skills was 27% (Zizys, 2011). The growth in mid-skill level jobs was only 9%, which suggests the emergence of a more bifurcated labour market with limited career pathways and progression opportunities. This shift in requirements for jobs is particularly significant for those trying to enter the labour market without a postsecondary certificate and for older workers who possess a limited range of transferable skills.

Almost a third of Canada's jobs fall into the categories of self-employed, fixed term or temporary. The post-recession period has not altered growth in these forms of employment which seemed to have peaked prior to the recession.

High rates of self-employment negatively affect overall coverage for Employment Insurance benefits and training programmes. Statistics Canada's 2013 Survey of Employment Insurance Coverage found that of the 1.312 million unemployed in Canada, 37.5% had not contributed to the Employment Insurance programme and as a result were ineligible. Of the non-contributors, 493 000 (88%) had not worked in the last 12 months. Of the 820 000 contributors, 536 000 or 85.8% were eligible to receive benefits. In Canada access to extended job search support and training is for the most part associated with EI eligibility. Only about 59.2% of clients have access to basic services and among these, over half (55%) would not have worked in the last 12 months.

Indigenous employment and economic development

Statistics Canada reports that 1 400 685 people had an indigenous identity in 2011, representing 4.3% of the total Canadian population (Statistics Canada, 2011). Indigenous Peoples accounted for 3.8% of the population enumerated in the 2006 Census, 3.3% in the 2001 Census and 2.8% in the 1996 Census. The indigenous population increased by 232 385 people, or 20.1% between 2006-11 compared to 5.2% for the non-indigenous population. It is estimated that the indigenous population will continue to grow at a faster rate than the non-indigenous population in the coming years, and could increase to between 2 million and 2.6 million (representing between 4.6%-6.1% of the total population respectively), by 2036 (Statistics Canada, 2015b).

Three main constitutionally recognised groups represent Canada's indigenous peoples: Indian, Métis, and Inuit. Indigenous and Northern Affairs Canada provides some guidance on definition and their use in its glossary

- The term **First Nations** came into common usage by late 1970s and 1980s as another term for the word "Indian". Although the term First Nation is widely used, no legal definition of it exists. Among its uses, the term "First Nations peoples" refers to "Indian" as defined in the "Indian Act". Some communities have also adopted the term "First Nation" to replace the word "band" in the name of their community. There are 618 First Nation communities in Canada as reported by Indigenous Affairs – 70 of which are located in Saskatchewan and 16 in the Yukon.
- **Inuit** are the indigenous people in Northern Canada, who predominately live in Nunavut, Northwest Territories, Northern Quebec and Northern Labrador. The word means "people" in the Inuit language – Inuktitut. The singular of Inuit is Inuk. There are no Inuit communities covered in this study.
- **Métis** are people of mixed First Nation and European ancestry who identify themselves as Métis, as distinct from First Nations people, Inuit or non-indigenous people. The Métis have a unique culture that draws on their diverse ancestral origins, such as Scottish, French, Ojibway and Cree. Métis are not expressly covered by this study but are included in statistics and programmes for indigenous people in the case study areas.

In 2011, 851 560 people identified as a First Nations person (includes both status and non-status Indians), representing 60.8% of the total indigenous population and 2.6% of the total Canadian population. 451 795 people identified as Métis. They represented 32.3% of the total indigenous population and 1.4% of the total Canadian population. While indigenous peoples in Yukon are overwhelmingly First Nations, Saskatchewan has a large Métis population (52 450) in addition to a significant First Nations population (103 205), representing 5.2% and 10.2% of the provinces population respectively. By 2036, the indigenous population could reach between 18.5% and 22.7% of the population in Saskatchewan, and between 21.7% and 24.6% in Yukon (Statistics Canada, 2015b).

The indigenous population is young with indigenous children aged 14 and under representing up 28.0% of the total indigenous population and indigenous youth aged 15 to 24 representing 18.2% of the total. Although it is estimated that the indigenous population will remain younger than the non-indigenous population by 2036, the former is expected to age more rapidly (Statistics Canada, 2015b).

Indigenous Peoples and the labour market

Labour market information (LMI) on Indigenous Peoples – First Nations, Métis and Inuit – is available through a number of sources including the Labour Force Survey, the Aboriginal Peoples Survey, the National Household Survey and the Census (ESDC, 2013b; INAC, 2013). However, the first two surveys exclude the indigenous population living on-reserve, which creates a major gap in the indigenous LMI. According to the National Household Survey, there were just over 1 million indigenous people aged 15 years or older living in Canada in 2011. The share of Indigenous Peoples among the population for each Canadian province and territory is shown in Figure 1.7.

Figure 1.7. **Share of Indigenous people aged 15 years or more, Canadian provinces, 2011**

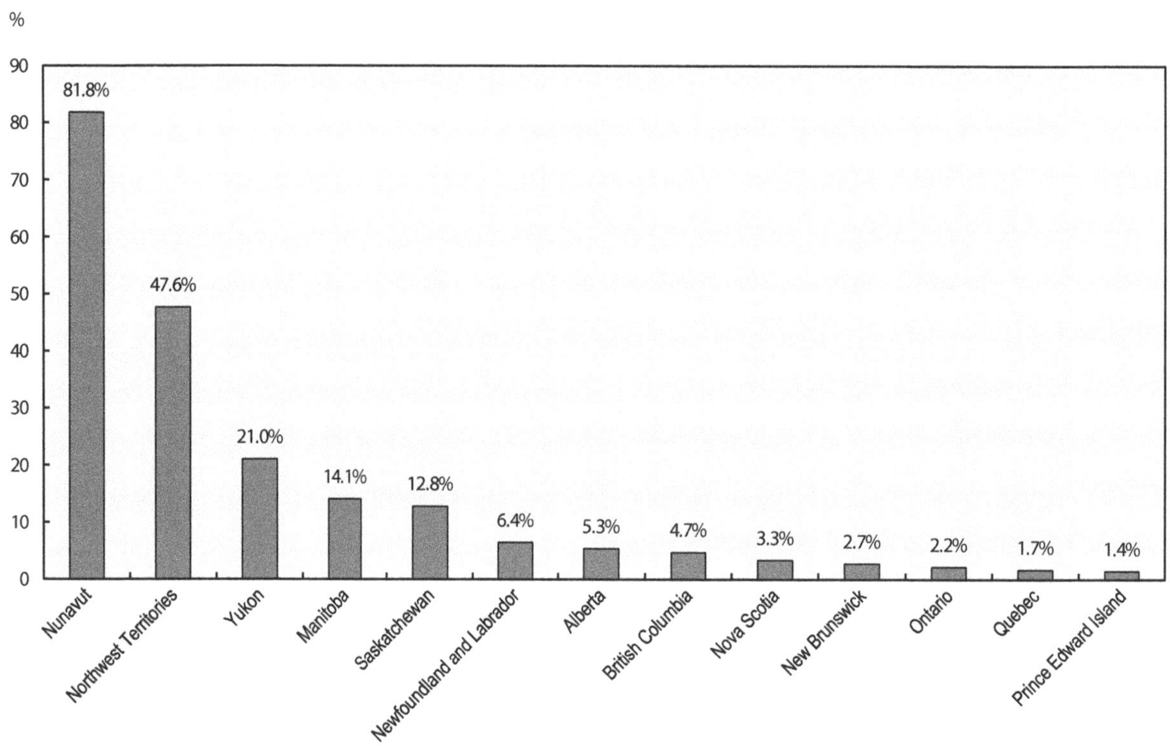

Source: Statistics Canada, 2011 National Household Survey, Statistics Canada Catalogue No. 99-011-X2011027.

Education and skills

According to the 2011 NHS, educational attainment for the indigenous population aged 15 or older lags behind the general population with 38% having no certificate, diploma or degree compared to 19% for non-indigenous individuals of the same age (Statistics Canada, 2013). In 2006, these figures were 44% and 23% respectively. The working age (25-64 year old) indigenous population increased by 21% between 2006-11 to reach 671 380, of whom 481 330 (or 72%) participated in the labour force.

By comparison, the number of other Canadians in this age group increased by only 5% between 2006-11, making indigenous people one of the most significant growth components in Canada's labour force. In 2011, the employment rate of the working age population was significantly lower for indigenous people at 63% compared with 76% for the non-indigenous population and the unemployment rate (13%) was more than double that of the rest of the working age population (6.0%). NHS data also show that, in 2011, educational attainment of indigenous people aged 15 or older was significantly lower than that of the rest of the Canadian population (Figure 1.8).

Figure 1.8. **Educational attainment, Indigenous and non-Indigenous populations aged 15 years or more, Canada, 2011**

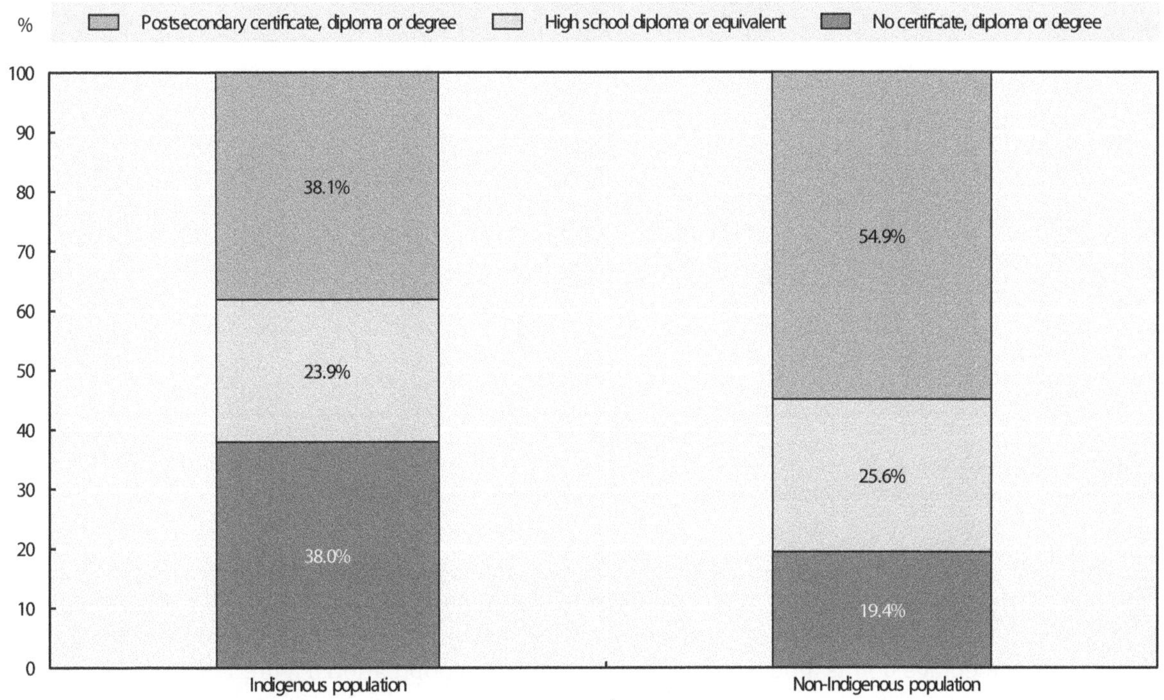

Note: This data only reflects provinces.
Source: Statistics Canada, 2011 National Household Survey, Statistics Canada Catalogue No. 99-012-X2011046.

Younger indigenous people had on average higher levels of educational attainment than older ones, with 74.1% of people aged 35 to 44 years holding at least a high school diploma compared to 66.4% of people aged 55 to 64 years (Statistics Canada, 2011). Indigenous women had higher levels of qualification than indigenous men and educational attainment was greater among Métis people, with 54.8% of 25 to 64 year olds having completed postsecondary education compared to 44.8% of First Nations people and 35.6% of Inuit individuals.

According to the results of the 2012 OECD Programme for the International Assessment of Adult Competencies (PIAAC[1]), literacy scores of Indigenous Peoples were on average lower than that of non-Indigenous peoples, with larger gaps observed in the three territories and in the province of Saskatchewan (Figure 1.9). Similar trends are observed in terms of numeracy scores.

Labour market trends

The labour market downturn that followed the 2008 economic crisis saw the gap between indigenous and non-indigenous populations widen in terms of unemployment, employment and participation rate (Usalcas, 2010). According to LFS data, the number of

Figure 1.9. **Average literacy scores, population aged 16 to 65, selected Canadian provinces and territories, 2012**

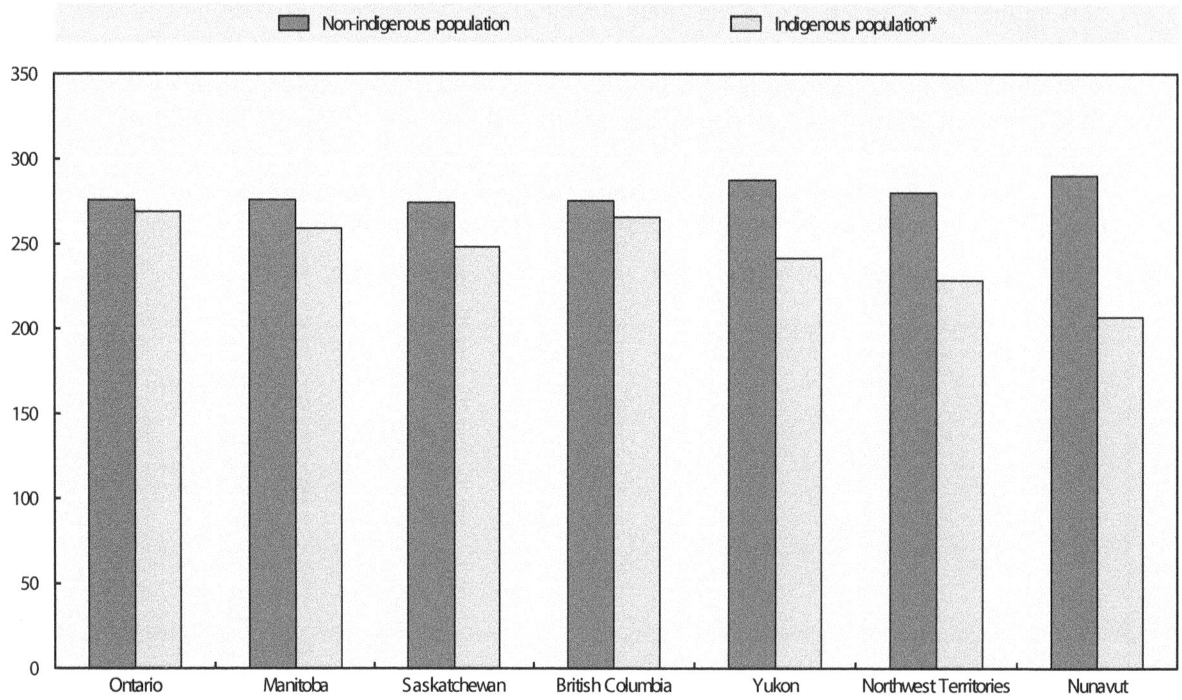

* Excluding people living on-reserve.
Source: The Programme for the International Assessment of Adult Competencies, 2012. See Table B.3.1.

indigenous people in employment fell by 1.2% between 2008-10, whereas job losses suffered by non-indigenous people in 2008-09 were almost recouped in 2011. Between 2008-09, the indigenous unemployment rate increased by 3.5 percentage points compared to 2.2 percentage points among the rest of the Canadian population (Figure 1.10).

However, the gap between the unemployment rates among these two populations decreased in recent years from a maximum of 6.2 percentage points in 2010 to 4.4 percentage points in 2014. However, the gap widened to 5.6 points in 2015. It is striking to note that unemployment rates among both groups are still persistently higher than they were in 2008, although they have improved since 2009-10. The unemployment rate among young Indigenous Peoples aged 15 to 24 years old peaked at 22.5% in 2009 (15.1% in the non-indigenous population), fell to 16.7% in 2014 (13.4% in the non-indigenous population), but increased again in 2015 to reach 18.8%, while it continued to fall in the non-indigenous population at 13%.

As shown in Table 1.1 below, the indigenous employment and participation rates were 6.2 and 2.9 percentage points lower than the non-Indigenous rates. Women had a lower unemployment rate in both the indigenous and non- indigenous population. The gender gap in terms of employment and participation rates was larger in the Canadian population as a whole than among the indigenous population. On average, indigenous workers tended to be paid less per hour worked in 2015 (23.31 CAD vs 25.24 CAD for non-indigenous workers).

Also when looking at provincial differences, the unemployment rate was higher and the employment rate lower among the indigenous population in all Canadian provinces (Figure 5.5 and 5.6), the widest gaps being observed in Saskatchewan for both indicators.

Figure 1.10. **Unemployment rate percentage of Indigenous and non-indigenous populations, Canada (excluding territories), 2007-15**

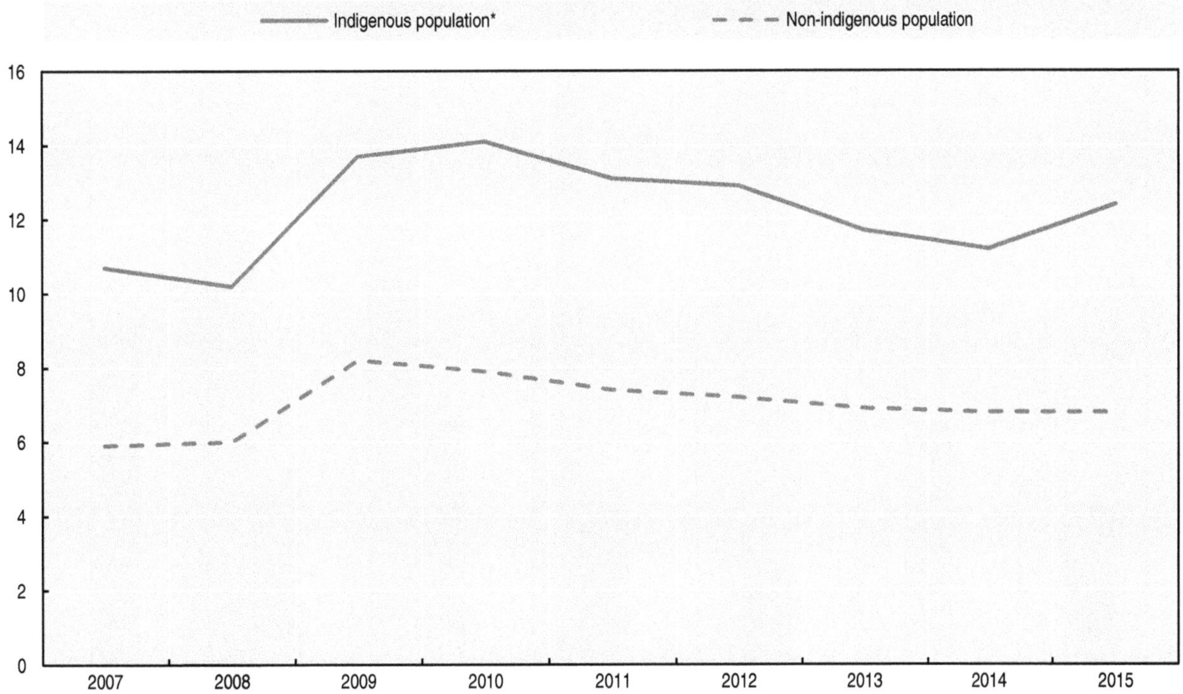

* Excluding people living on-reserve.
Source: Statistics Canada. Table 282-0226 – Labour force survey estimates (LFS).

Table 1.1. **Unemployment, employment and participation rate, percentage of Indigenous and non-indigenous populations aged 15 years or more, Canada (excluding territories), 2015**

	Unemployment rate			Employment rate			Participation rate		
	Women	Men	Total	Women	Men	Total	Women	Men	Total
Non-indigenous population	6.1	7.3	6.8	57.5	65.5	61.4	61.3	70.7	65.9
Indigenous population*	11.7	13.1	12.4	52.3	58.3	55.2	59.2	67.1	63.0

* Excluding people living on-reserve.
Source: Statistics Canada. Table 282-0226 – Labour force survey estimates (LFS).

Employment by industry

In 2014, there were a greater number of indigenous people employed in the goods-producing sectors (23.6% vs 21.8%) and fewer employed in services sectors (76.4% vs 78.2%) compared to the non-indigenous population (Statistics Canada, 2014).

The largest shares of employment for indigenous people were in trade (15.3%), health care and social assistance (13.6%) and construction (10.9%). This population was particularly over-represented in construction, accommodation and food services and public administration, and under-represented in professional, scientific and technical services, manufacturing, and finance, insurance, real estate and leasing.

Indigenous women were significantly more employed in services industries (91.9% vs 61.1% for men) and less employed in goods-producing industries (8.1% vs 38.9%). Indigenous men were mostly employed in construction, trade and manufacturing, while

Figure 1.11. **Unemployment rate, percentage of indigenous and non-indigenous populations aged 15 years or more, Canadian provinces (excluding territories), 2014**

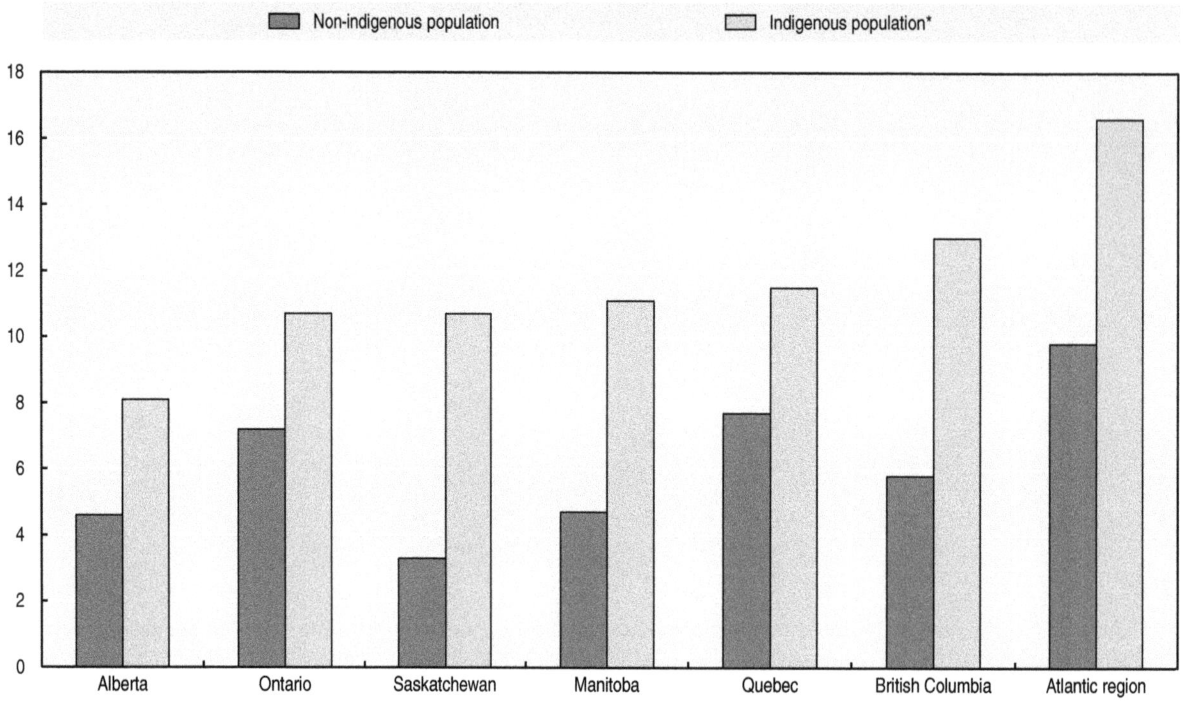

* Excluding people living on-reserve.
Source: Statistics Canada. Table 282-0226 – Labour force survey estimates (LFS).

Figure 1.12. **Employment rate, percentage of indigenous and non-indigenous populations aged 15 years or more, Canadian provinces (excluding territories), December 2014**

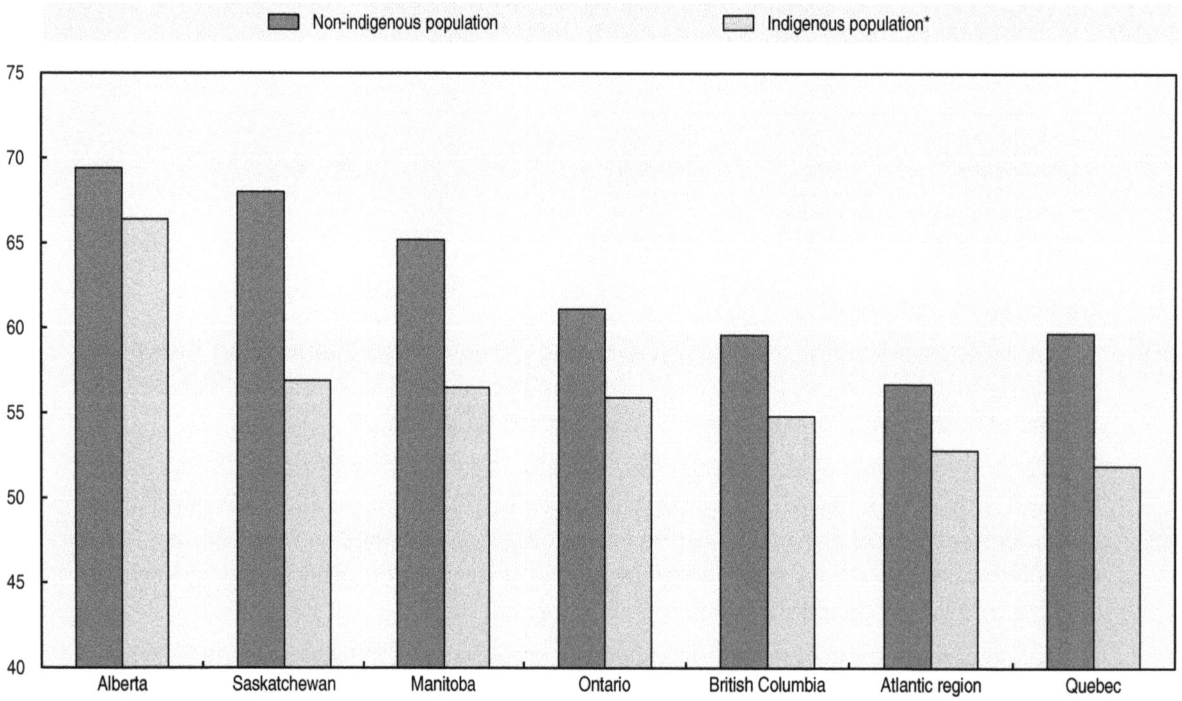

* Excluding people living on-reserve.
Source: Statistics Canada. Table 282-0226 – Labour force survey estimates (LFS).

women mainly in health care and social assistance, trade, and accommodation and food services. The gender difference in terms of sector of employment is more pronounced for indigenous than for non- indigenous people.

Employment by occupations

In 2014, the largest shares of employment for indigenous people were in sales and service (30.3%) and in trades, transport and equipment operators (20.4%), two occupations in which this population was over-represented in comparison with the rest of the Canadian population (Statistics Canada, 2015c). Conversely, indigenous people were under-represented in occupations in natural and applied sciences, and in business, finance and administrative occupations. Significant gender differences could be observed also in terms of occupation, with the largest number of jobs being in sales and service occupations for indigenous women (39% vs 21.8% for men) and in trades, transport and equipment operators for indigenous men (38.1% vs 2.5% for women).

Indigenous businesses and entrepreneurship

In 2014, approximately 40 000 indigenous workers were registered as self-employed in Canada, which represented 8.7% of total indigenous employment (Statistics Canada, 2015c). While this proportion remained lower than in the non-indigenous population (15.4%), the growth of self-employment has been significantly higher within the indigenous population (+10.7% vs +1.4% in the non-indigenous population) between 2011-14.

According to the Canadian Council for Aboriginal Business (CCAB, 2011), while the majority of businesses owned by Métis and Inuit people were located off-reserve in 2011, 72% of First Nations-owned businesses were located on-reserve. The largest proportions of indigenous-owned businesses were in the construction and primary sectors, but impressive growth in indigenous entrepreneurship in knowledge-based industries has been observed in recent years. Given that around 40% of indigenous self-employed business owners employ other people, entrepreneurship can be a crucial factor for stimulating job creation within and outside indigenous communities. Limited access to capital in order to start a business and lack of business skills and formal training have been identified as the main barriers to self-employment within indigenous populations (Statistics Canada, 2015c).

Note

1. More information on the PIAAC survey is available on the following website: *www.oecd.org/site/piaac/*.

References

Abele, F. and S. Delic (2014), *Aboriginal Youth Employment in Northern Canada*, Carleton Centre for Community Innovation, Knowledge Synthesis Report R# 14-01.

Bernard, A. (2015), "Youth Labour Force Participation: 2008 to 2014", *Economic Insights*, No. 052, Statistics Canada, Catalogue No. 11-626-X, ISBN 978-0-660-03522-2.

Bernard, A. (2013), "Unemployment Dynamics Among Canada's Youth", *Economic Insights*, No. 024, Statistics Canada, Catalogue No. 11-626-X, ISBN 978-1-100-22298-1.

CCAB (2011), "Promise and Prosperity: Aboriginal Business Survey", Canadian Council for Aboriginal Business, *www.ccab.com/uploads/File/Promise-and-Prosperity--The-Aboriginal-Business-Survey.pdf*.

Cross, P. (2015), *Serving up the Reality of Youth Unemployment*, Macdonald-Laurier Institute, Ottawa.

ESDC (2013a), "Canadian Occupational Projection System Projections", Employment and Social Development Canada.

ESDC (2013b), *Aboriginal Labour Market Bulletin*, Volume 2, Issue 2, Employment and Social Development Canada.

INAC (2013), "Fact Sheet – 2011 National Household Survey Aboriginal Demographics, Educational Attainment and Labour Market Outcomes", Indigenous and Northern Affairs Canada.

OECD (2016), "GDP per capita and productivity growth", *OECD Productivity Statistics* (database), *http://dx.doi.org/10.1787/data-00685-en*, (accessed on 24 February 2016).

OECD (2016), "Regional demography", *OECD Regional Statistics* (database). *http://dx.doi.org/10.1787/a8f15243-en.*

OECD (2015a), "OECD Economic Outlook No. 98 (Edition 2015/2)", *OECD Economic Outlook: Statistics and Projections* (database), *http://dx.doi.org/10.1787/bd810434-en.*

OECD (2015b), "Canada", in *Education at a Glance 2015: OECD Indicators*, OECD Publishing, Paris. *http://dx.doi.org/10.1787/eag-2015-47-en.*

OECD (2015c), "Multifactor productivity" (indicator), *http://dx.doi.org/10.1787/a40c5025-en.*

OECD (2014), *OECD Economic Surveys: Canada 2014*, OECD Publishing, Paris, *http://dx.doi.org/10.1787/eco_surveys-can-2014-en.*

RBC (2014), "Impact of Lower Oil Prices on the Canadian Economic Outlook: An Update", *Current Analysis*, December 2014, Royal Bank of Canada.

Statistics Canada (2015a), "Canada's population estimates: Age and sex, July 1, 2015", *The Daily*, September 29, Statistics Canada catalogue No. 11-001-X.

Statistics Canada (2015b), *Projections of the Aboriginal Population and Households in Canada, Catalogue No. 91-552-X,* ISSN 1927-6389.

Statistics Canada (2015c), *Aboriginal Labour Market Bulletin*, Volume 4, Issue 1.

Statistics Canada (2015d), "Job Vacancy and Wage Survey, first quarter 2015", *The Daily*, August 13. Statistics Canada, catalogue No. 11-001-X.

Statistics Canada (2013), "The educational attainment of Aboriginal peoples in Canada", *NHS in Brief*, Catalogue No. 99-012-X2011003.

Statistics Canada (2011), "Aboriginal Peoples in Canada: First Nations People, Métis and Inuit, National Household Survey", *www12.statcan.gc.ca/nhs-enm/2011/as-sa/99-011-x/99-011-x2011001-eng.cfm.*

Usalcas, J. (2010), "Aboriginal People and the Labour Market: Estimates from the Labour Force Survey, 2008-2010", *The Aboriginal Labour Force Analysis Series*, Statistics Canada – Catalogue No. 71-588-X, No. 3.

Zizys, T. (2011), *Working Better: Creating a High-Performing Labour Market in Ontario*, the Metcalf Foundation, Toronto, Canada.

Employment and Skills Strategies in Saskatchewan
and the Yukon, Canada

Chapter 2

Canadian federal employment policies and programmes

Employment and Social Development is the main department responsible for employment and skills policies in Canada. They work with other federal departments and provincial/territorial governments to implement a number of policies and programmes across Canada. Indigenous and Northern Affairs Canada plays a significant role in the management of employment and economic development policies targeted to Indigenous Peoples in Canada. This chapter provides an overview of key employment and skills programmes at the federal level, including those which are targeted to Indigenous Peoples.

Employment and skills programmes at the federal level

At the federal level, **Employment and Social Development Canada** (ESDC) holds primary responsibility for developing a skilled, adaptable and inclusive workforce, including leading the management of employment and labour market policy as well as management of training and skills development policy. Federal involvement in labour market policies and in training and skills development in particular stems from the federal responsibilities for the national economy and for jobs and growth. Federal involvement is also based on equity; training and skills development is an important lever to support the economic prospects of groups who face barriers to full participation in the labour market. Disadvantaged groups are also more vulnerable to economic shocks and to structural changes in the economy. In a context of population and workforce ageing the ongoing prosperity of countries depends on the optimal use of its human resources.

Canada's system is designed to provide financial support to unemployed Canadians while they look for work or upgrade their skills. The Employment Insurance (EI) system consists of two complementary components: temporary financial assistance (referred to as EI Part I); and employment support and training that unemployed Canadians need to find a job (referred to as EI Part II). EI Part I is delivered by the Government of Canada, while EI Part II is delivered by the provinces and territories.

The federal government is responsible for collecting premiums and providing stewardship over the EI Account. Both the **Canadian Employment Insurance Commission (CEIC)** and ESDC play a leadership role in overseeing the EI programme. For almost 75 years, this tripartite organisation has included representation from business, labour and the Government of Canada.

Part II of the EI Act provides for employment benefits for insured participants. EI Part II assists unemployed people return to employment with support measures (such as counselling and job search assistance) and benefits (such as skills development and work experience). Under bilateral Labour Market Development Agreements (LMDAs), over CAD 2 billion in EI funds are transferred to provinces and territories each year to design and deliver training programmes and employment assistance that meet local labour market needs. There is a legislative requirement that programmes delivered under the LMDAs must be "similar" to the EBSMs established by the Government of Canada. Employment Benefits, for EI-eligible clients (i.e., active and former claimants) include:

- Skills Development – which provides financial assistance to individuals to make their own arrangements to obtain skills for employment;
- Targeted Wage Subsidies – which encourages employers to hire persons they would not normally hire;
- Self-Employment – which helps individuals start their own businesses;
- Job Creation Partnerships – which provides individuals with opportunities to gain work experience leading to ongoing employment; and

- Targeted Earning Supplements – which encourages unemployed persons to accept employment by offering them temporary financial incentives.

An additional CAD 500 million from general tax revenues is transferred to provinces and territories to provide skills development and employment training with a focus on the unemployed with a low level of skills and education who are mainly not EI-eligible. Established in 2014, following the expiry of the Labour Market Agreements, the Canada Job Fund Agreements (CJFAs) include flexibilities to design and deliver programmes to meet local labour market needs, in alignment with core principles. CJFAs support a broad range of employment supports and services with priority given to the unemployed and low-skilled. This includes the Canada Job Grant that puts training decisions in the hands of employers and includes support for a range of employer-sponsored training initiatives.

The Labour Market Agreements for Persons with Disabilities (LMAPDs) are the federal government's single largest source of support to help persons with disabilities to enter and stay in the labour market. Under the LMAPDs CAD 222 million are allocated each year to the provinces and territories to determine their own priorities and approaches to best address the labour market needs of persons with disabilities.

In addition to Skills Development training under Part II of the EI Act, ESDC funds training in occupational and general skills from general revenues (the Consolidated Revenue Funds) for those who do not qualify for employment benefits. This includes training that is often incidental to programmes for groups with particular barriers to the labour market such as youth, older workers, immigrants and persons with disabilities. Funds from the CRF are also used for services for indigenous persons.

As well as transfers and collaborative arrangements, the Government of Canada invests and acts directly in federal labour market objectives that aim to preserve Canada's economic union. As such federal programming helps to address national labour market challenges, develops and maintains a national pool of skilled labour, supports mobility of labour across Canada, promotes opportunities for individuals with a focus on under-represented groups and minimises unemployment

The federal government manages a number of labour market policies and programmes that are preventative in nature. For example, to help avert job loss and detachment from the labour market, ESDC oversees the Work-Sharing (WS) programme that has a focus on unemployment prevention, by helping to avert job loss when there is a reduction in business activity. The programme provides income support in the form of employment insurance WS benefits to eligible workers who work a temporarily reduced work week while their employer recovers (i.e., returns to normal level of business activity). The goal is for all participating employees to return to normal working hours by the end of the term of the WS agreement. Employer sponsored skills enhancement, whether on-the-job training or off-site courses, may take place during the period of a WS agreement, however attendance would be optional.

Mobility of workers can help prevent unemployment. There are a number of federal policies that support mobility; removing barriers for workers to move to where there is demand for workers. **Canada Revenue Agency** allows eligible moving expenses for individuals who move and establish a new home to work or run a business at a new location, or to take courses as a student in full-time attendance enrolled in a postsecondary programme at a university, college or other educational institution. **Industry Canada** is responsible for the *Agreement on Internal Trade*, which makes it easier for people who work in regulated professions to get certified in other jurisdictions and work in their field. ESDC also supports labour mobility through labour market information products to help students, workers and employers anticipate the skills that will be needed in the future, and through Job Bank which offers national job matching for employers and job seekers.

The provision of Labour Market Information (LMI) is a major component of the skills agenda for the 21st Century adopted by the Labour Ministers. Better information on the labour market (such as data on wages, job openings, training opportunities and certification), is a critical element in helping Canadians acquire the skills needed to plan their careers in the new economy. The federal government has implemented a number of initiatives to ensure that Canadians have access to labour market information to know what jobs are available. Budget 2015 included commitments to launch a new one-stop shop national labour market information portal. Job Bank is an electronic listing of jobs provided by employers from everywhere across Canada. There are a number of functionalities within Job Bank including job match, career planning tools, vacancy and wage information.

The federal government has made contributions to postsecondary education for many years. This support is now included under the Canada Social Transfer (CST). Under the CST, the federal government provides funding to provincial and territorial governments for postsecondary education, health care and other social programmes.

Student loans in Canada help postsecondary students pay for their education. The federal government funds the **Canada Student Loan Program** (CSLP) which provides financial assistance in the form of loans and grants to postsecondary students who demonstrate financial need. Provinces and territories may fund their own programmes or initiatives that run in parallel with the CSLP. The federal government also provides a range of tax-related credits and saving incentives to help students and their families pay for their postsecondary education.

Apprenticeships

Canadian workers may opt to enrol in apprenticeship programmes, which combine workplace learning with classroom instruction. According to the Canadian Apprenticeship Forum (CAF) the training combines alternating periods of on-the-job (80 to 85%) and technical training (15 to 20%). After completing both the classroom and the on-the-job training, apprentices can receive journeyperson certification or a certificate of qualification. Depending on the trade, it takes about two to five years as an apprentice to become a certified journeyperson. Each province and territory has its own training and certification policies and its own list of designated apprenticeship programmes.

The federal government works closely with provinces and territories to manage and deliver the Interprovincial Standards Red Seal Program which promotes a set of common standards that allow the recognition of certifications across provincial jurisdictions. While professional certificates or licenses are recognised by all provincial jurisdictions under the Agreement on Internal Trade (AIT), the Red Seal provides the assurance that workers are qualified according to common standards of knowledge and competency as defined by industry. Through the Red Seal Program, examinations are developed and maintained through a rigorous industry-driven process for 56 Red Seal trades. The federal government also provides a range of programmes and services to help apprentices in their certification process. Apprentices can apply for the Canada Apprentice Loan and other financial supports like grants and tax credits.

The Canadian Council of Directors of Apprenticeship (CCDA) is responsible for the management of the Red Seal Program. The CCDA works with industry to facilitate the development of a skilled labour force, and labour mobility across Canada. Total registered apprenticeship numbers in Canada more than doubled between 1991-2009, rising from 192 945 to reach 409 038 registrations (Skof, 2011).

Labour market initiatives targeted to specific groups

Youth

The Youth Employment Strategy (YES) is the Government of Canada's suite of employment programmes for youth. Delivered through Employment and Social Development Canada, over CAD 330 million is invested annually to help young people between the ages of 15-30 get the information and gain the skills, job experience and abilities they need to make a successful transition to the workplace. Specifically, the YES offers three initiatives: Skills Link, Career Focus, and the Summer Work Experience programme.

Skills Link helps young people who face more barriers to employment than others develop basic employability skills and gain valuable job experience to assist them in making a successful transition into the labour market or to return to school. They could be youth who have not completed high school, single parents, indigenous youth, young persons with disabilities, youth living in rural or remote areas or recent immigrants.

Career Focus helps postsecondary graduates transition to the labour market through paid internships, and helps to provide youth with the information and experience they need to make informed career decisions, find a job and/or pursue advanced studies. This includes full-time internships for postsecondary graduates in high-demand fields such as science, technology, engineering, mathematics and the skilled trades and supporting internships in small and medium-sized enterprises

Summer Work Experience provides wage subsidies to employers to create summer employment for secondary and postsecondary students. The Summer Work Experience programme includes Canada Summer Jobs (CSJ). CSJ provides funding for not-for-profit organisations, public-sector employers, and small businesses with 50 or fewer employees to create summer job opportunities for students.

The YES is currently being improved to provide youth with more practical and real-life work experience, and to help youth make more informed career choices that prepare them for the transition into the labour force. Starting in 2015-16, for two years, targeted programming will support the relocation of youth and immigrants to areas where job opportunities exist.

The Government of Canada also provides significant support to Skills Canada to actively promote careers in skilled trades and technologies to Canadian youth by working with local organisations, educators and governments.

Indigenous Peoples

Under Canada's constitution the federal government has primary responsibility for Indigenous Peoples. Indigenous and Northern Affairs Canada (INAC) is the lead federal government department responsible for monitoring the implementation of the Government of Canada's obligations and commitments to First Nations, Inuit and Métis, and the fulfilment of the federal government's constitutional responsibilities in the North. Numerous statutes, negotiated agreements and relevant legal decisions largely determine the Department's responsibilities. Most of its programmes, representing a majority of its spending – are delivered through partnerships with indigenous communities and federal-provincial or federal-territorial agreements. INAC also serves urban indigenous people, as well as Métis and Inuit, of which many reside in rural areas.

The Department is also responsible for implementing its approximately 2 100 treaty obligations under comprehensive land claim and self-government agreements, as well as coordinating the implementation of over 4 000 obligations for all of Canada flowing from these agreements (Government of Canada, 1999, 1993 and 1985).

INAC also provides support for services on reserves such as education, housing, community infrastructure and social support to Status Indians and Band members on reserves; administers the land management component of the Indian Act; and executes other regulatory duties under the Indian Act. A First Nations community may operate entirely or partially under the Indian Act, or it may be self-governing. As mentioned, self-government agreements are one means of building sound governance and institutional capacity that allow indigenous communities to contribute to, and participate in, the decisions that affect their lives and carry out effective relationships with other governments. Self-government agreements give indigenous groups greater control and law-making authority over a comprehensive range of jurisdictions, including governance, social and economic development, education, health and lands.

INAC negotiates comprehensive and specific claims on behalf of the Government of Canada. Specific claims deal with the past grievances of First Nations. These grievances relate to Canada's obligations under historic treaties or the way it managed First Nation funds or assets. Comprehensive land claims, on the other hand, generally arise in areas of Canada where indigenous land rights have not been dealt with by treaty or through other legal means. In these areas, these agreements (also called "modern treaties") are negotiated between the indigenous group, Canada, and the province or territory, and provide certainty about the ownership, use and management of land and resources for all parties. This creates an environment that is more conducive to resource development and other economic development opportunities, and studies point to better socio-economic outcomes for indigenous groups who have completed comprehensive land claims.

As well, INAC negotiates self-government agreements on behalf of the Government of Canada. The negotiation of self-government creates a forum for Canada to have a meaningful dialogue with indigenous communities. Negotiation of self-government agreements foster a renewed, nation-to-nation relationship based on trust, respect, and a true spirit of co-operation and partnership. These self-government agreements can either be negotiated as part of a comprehensive land claim, or they can be negotiated as stand-alone or sectoral self-government agreements. Self-government agreements provide clarity regarding the legal regime and related questions of authority and accountability for decision making, which fosters greater community pride and increases investor confidence, supporting economic partnerships and improving living conditions. As a result, greater prosperity for indigenous people and a more promising future for all Canadians may be achieved. In fact, government and academic studies suggest self-governing indigenous communities have better education, employment and labour force participation rates, and higher income levels than Indigenous groups without self-government arrangements.

First Nations may choose to opt out of 34 land-related sections of the *Indian Act* and develop their own land codes in order to govern reserve lands and resources – and take advantage of economic development opportunities. This option is made possible through the First Nations Land Management Regime, which transfers administration of land to a participating First Nation. This includes the authority to enact laws with respect to land, the environment, and most resources. There are currently 96 active First Nations in First Nations Land Management Regime. There are 54 operating under their land code and 41 in the developmental phase (developing their land codes).

Canada has signed 22 self-government agreements recognizing a wide range of indigenous jurisdictions that involve 36 indigenous communities across Canada. Of those, 18 are part of a comprehensive land claim agreement (modern treaty). Eleven of those comprehensive land claim and self-government agreements are with First Nations in the Yukon. Two self-governing First Nations' traditional territories (the Kwalin Dün and the Ta'an Kwäch'än) are where Whitehorse was established, and they have lands within the municipality of Whitehorse. Dawson City was built on the traditional lands of the Tr'ondëk Hwëch'in First Nation and the First Nation still have lands within the municipality. In Saskatchewan, Canada is also in the process of negotiating a self-government agreement with Whitecap Dakota First Nation

Education Programmes

The Government of Canada funds elementary and secondary education for First Nations students ordinarily resident on reserve, and provides postsecondary education financial support for eligible First Nation and Inuit students. INAC works with First Nations and the provinces/territories to support quality education for First Nations students so they can acquire the skills needed to enter the labour market and be full participants in the Canadian economy.

The **Elementary and Secondary Education Program** provides eligible students ordinarily living on-reserve with elementary and secondary education programmes comparable to those in provincial schools. For students who live on-reserve but attend school off-reserve, INAC pays the tuition amount charged by the province.

The **Education Partnerships Program (EPP)** is a proposal-based programme designed to promote collaboration between First Nations, provinces, INAC and other stakeholders. The programme supports the establishment and advancement of formal partnership arrangements that develop practical working relationships between officials and educators in provincial systems and regional First Nation organisations and schools.

The **First Nation Student Success Program (FNSSP)** is designed to support First Nation educators on-reserve (kindergarten to grade 12) in their ongoing efforts to meet students' needs and improve student and school results. In particular, the programme supports activities that increase student achievement levels in reading and writing (literacy), mathematics (numeracy) and encourage students to remain in school (student retention).

The **New Paths for Education Program** funds projects and activities that improve the quality of education in First Nation schools and enhance the educational experiences of students, teachers, administrators, parents and communities. These include professional development for teachers, curriculum development, involvement of parents in children's education and more.

The **High-Cost Special Education Program** funds band-operated schools for high-cost special education students assessed with moderate to profound learning disabilities The High-Cost Special Education Program is designed to help eligible students to access quality programmes and services that are culturally sensitive and reflective of generally accepted provincial/territorial standards. Students identified as having mild to moderate learning disabilities are supported through the Elementary and Secondary Education Program.

The **Postsecondary Student Support Program (PSSSP)** provides funding (through recipient organisations/Band Councils) to First Nation and eligible Inuit students enrolled in eligible postsecondary programmes. The programme aims to improve the employability of First Nation and Inuit students by providing them with funding to access education and skills development opportunities at the postsecondary level.

The **University and College Entrance Preparation Program (UCEPP)** provides financial assistance to First Nation and eligible Inuit students enrolled in university or college entrance programmes to help them gain the academic level required to enter a degree or diploma programme.

The **Postsecondary Partnerships Program (PSPP)** provides funding to eligible Canadian postsecondary institutions to design and deliver university- and college-level courses tailored for First Nations and eligible Inuit students. These courses help students gain the skills they need to enter and succeed in the labour market. Indspire is an Indigenous-led charity that invests in the education of indigenous people for the long-term benefit of these individuals, their families and communities and Canada. INAC provides funds to Indspire to:

- Offer scholarships and bursaries to First Nation and Inuit students to pursue postsecondary education
- Identify and honour the outstanding achievements of First Nation and Inuit people so that their accomplishments can serve as an inspiration to young people
- Hold youth career fairs, targeted at indigenous youth from grades to 10 to 12, in two different Canadian cities each year

Other education initiatives

The Government of Canada also negotiates self-government as a mechanism to improve education outcomes. The Mi'kmaq Education Agreement is a promising example of these improvements. This agreement conferred law-making authority to its 12 Nova Scotia First Nations signatories, and created a new organisation to administer its member communities' schools. These communities have seen notable improvements in student outcomes, and in 2014-15 achieved a graduation rate of 89.6%, comparable to the provincial average of 92.5% (INAC, 2013). The Government of Canada has also signed a Tripartite Education Framework Agreement with the First Nations Education Steering Committee (FNESC) and the province of British Columbia in January 2012. The Agreement recognizes that FNESC has the capacity and responsibility for administering second level services to participating First Nations and First Nation schools in British Columbia, and is supported by a new funding model that funds First Nation schools on reserve in the same way as similarly sized and situated provincial public schools. The Agreement:

- Outlines the standards, programmes, services and school supports which address the unique needs of First Nation students;
- Supports the delivery of quality education programmes and services meeting standards that allow First Nation students to transfer without academic penalty, at similar levels of achievement, between First Nation schools and provincial schools;

- Recognises FNESC and First Nations have worked to establish an education system to support First Nation students and schools that reflects the values and traditions of the communities they serve;
- Recognises FNESC has demonstrated the capacity to administer education programmes and second level services on behalf of First Nations and First Nation schools in BC;
- Is supported by a new funding model for participating BC First Nations that will fund First Nation schools on reserve in the same way as similarly sized and situated BC public schools.

Several other First Nations have either negotiated, or are currently negotiating, jurisdiction over education as part of either a combined comprehensive land claim and self-government agreement, or a stand-alone self-government agreement. Examples of some indigenous groups with completed agreements that include jurisdiction over education are: Westbank First Nation, Nisga'a Lisims First Nation, and Sioux Valley Dakota Nation. In some cases, where agreements have been completed, communities have not opted to operate their own education systems, and instead have worked on a government-to-government basis with the province to have their students educated in provincial schools. Examples of indigenous groups currently negotiating jurisdiction over self-government include: the Union of Ontario Indians, the Mowhawk Council of Akwesasne, Whitecap Dakota First Nation, and Miawpukek First Nation.

Economic development and employment

Indigenous and Northern Affairs Canada is the lead federal department for the management of economic development policies for indigenous peoples. The management of economic development policies is composed of the following policy and programme areas: Aboriginal Entrepreneurship, Community Economic Development, Strategic Partnerships, Infrastructure and Capacity, Administration of Reserve Land, and Urban Aboriginal Participation. The management and implementation of various Treaties and Agreements between the Crown and Aboriginal peoples includes an important economic development component.

Through its Northern Development mandate, INAC is the lead federal department for two-fifths of Canada's landmass, with a direct role in the political and economic development of the territories, and significant responsibilities for science, land, and environmental management. In the North, the territorial governments generally provide the majority of social programmes and services to all Northerners, including indigenous peoples. Other federal government departments and agencies such as the Canadian Northern Economic Development Agency (CanNor) also play major roles in the development of the North.

The following is a description of the programmes and policy areas within INAC in the management of economic development policies.

- The Aboriginal Entrepreneurship Program supports the creation and growth of viable indigenous businesses by facilitating increased access to business capital, support services and business opportunities. In playing this key support role, the programme seeks to influence the longer-term viability of indigenous business, leading to improved economic prosperity for indigenous Canadians.
- The Community Economic Development Program enhances the value of indigenous assets, by supporting activities that promote the underlying conditions for economic

development. In playing this key support role, Community Economic Development programming expects to promote greater self-reliance and participation in the mainstream economy, and community well-being.

- The Strategic Partnerships is an innovative horizontal initiative intended to align federal efforts to enhance Aboriginal participation in complex economic development opportunities, particularly for engaging larger regional economic investment opportunities and/or potential major resource development. The programme provides a mechanism for federal partners to collectively identify these emerging opportunities, target investment decisions, and streamline the necessary programme applications and approval processes to support and enhance indigenous communities' engagement at the earliest stages of large and complex economic development opportunities. In the process, this approach helps build closer partnerships with non-federal partners, including provincial and territorial governments, the private sector, and indigenous communities. Thus, the programme serves to align all federal government efforts in leveraging investments from other levels of government and the private sector, and addressing gaps in programming, to ensure indigenous Canadians can participate in and benefit from priority regional opportunities and major resource developments.
- The Infrastructure and capacity programme supports First Nation communities in acquiring, constructing, owning, operating and maintaining a base infrastructure that protects their health and safety and enables their engagement in the economy. The sub-programmes provide funding and advice to support housing, capacity building, and community infrastructure, including water and wastewater systems, education facilities, roads and bridges, electrification, and community buildings.
- The Northern Land, Resources and Environmental Management Program focuses on the management, sustainable development and regulatory oversight of the land, water, natural resources, and environment of the North, delivering on INAC's role as the Government of Canada's natural resource manager in Nunavut and the offshore, and its post-devolution responsibilities in the Northwest Territories and Yukon. This programme involves managing oil and gas resources development; supporting the sustainable management of active mineral exploration and development; supporting the sound management of contaminated sites, Nunavut and the few remaining department-managed land and water areas in the North; and ensuring the completion of territorial land-use planning, including zones for conservation, development and other uses.

Labour markets and skills training

Economic development and job creation for indigenous people is an important priority, guided by the Federal Framework for Aboriginal Economic Development. INAC works with ESDC in developing indigenous human capital. An estimated 350 000 Indigenous youth will turn 15 years old between 2016-26 (Statistics Canada, 2015), which provides an unprecedented opportunity to leverage investments in job and skills training and employment readiness for indigenous youth in order to fill crucial labour shortages (ESDC, 2013).

ESDC funds indigenous labour market programmes to increase workforce participation and to help indigenous people prepare for, find, and keep jobs. Indigenous agreement holders deliver these programmes across Canada. Additionally, through the Skills and Partnership Fund, ESDC provides skills and employment training for in-demand jobs. This fund helps indigenous organisations partner with government, business, and local community organisations to improve skills training and create job opportunities. Projects focus largely, though not exclusively, on training for specific job vacancies in high demand sectors (e.g. trades, mining and energy).

Through the indigenous labour market programmes, ESDC provides skills and employment training to increase workforce participation and help First Nations, Métis and Inuit people prepare for, find and maintain jobs.

The Aboriginal Skills and Employment Training Strategy provides a suite of skills development and training from essential skills acquisition (e.g. literacy and numeracy) to more advanced training-to-employment programming for indigenous people across the country. Funding is provided to a network of 84 indigenous organisations that design and deliver programmes and services through over 600 points of service across the country.

The Skills and Partnership Fund is a partnership-based, opportunity driven programme targeting job training and skills development for indigenous people so they may fill specific job vacancies in high demand sectors such as natural resource development and the digital economy.

The First Nations Jobs Fund is a component of the on-reserve Income Assistance Reform and provides personalised job training and support to young on-reserve income assistance recipients in participating communities to help them connect with available jobs. The First Nations Job Fund is delivered by the Aboriginal Skills and Employment Training Strategy network.

Indigenous and Northern Affairs Canada also addresses labour market participation by investing in the Aboriginal Capacity Development Program administered by the National Aboriginal Capital Corporation Association. The programme supports the training activities of Aboriginal Financial Institution staff on the effective and consistent delivery of developmental lending and business support services for indigenous entrepreneurs. The Department's Procurement Strategy for Aboriginal Business also encourages the participation of indigenous businesses and labour force in the economy.

The Aboriginal Economic Development Program within INAC aims to build and promote viable Indigenous businesses and opportunity-ready communities. This programme supports the vision of increasing the participation of indigenous individuals and communities in the Canadian economy and enabling indigenous people to pursue the same opportunities for employment, income and wealth creation as other Canadians.

Through the Income Assistance Reform, Indigenous and Northern Affairs Canada and Employment and Social Development Canada work together to connect Income Assistance clients aged between 18-24 with skills training and jobs. This programme supports the capacity of First Nation service providers in providing individualised case management and provides clients with a range of pre-employment, counselling interventions and skills training.

The Youth Employment Strategy is the Government of Canada's commitment to help young people, particularly those facing barriers to employment, get the information and gain the skills, work experience and abilities they need to make a successful transition into the labour market. INAC is one of eleven federal Departments which deliver programming in support of the Strategy. The First Nations and Inuit Youth Employment Strategy (FNIYES) supports initiatives to provide First Nations and Inuit youth with work experience, information about career options, and opportunities to develop skills to help gain employment and develop careers. This strategy includes two programmes: the First

Nations and Inuit Summer Work Experience Program and the First Nations and Inuit Skills Link Program.

The First Nations and Inuit Summer Work Experience Program provides youth with employment opportunities where they can gain work experience and develop important skills such as communication, problem-solving and teamwork. Summer work placements allow youth to learn about career options and to earn income that may contribute to university or college education.

The First Nations and Inuit Skills Link Program supports initiatives that assist young people in acquiring the essential skills that will help them gain employment, function well in the workplace and learn about job and career options. The programme also promotes the benefits of education to future participation in the labour force

Urban Indigenous People

Nearly 50% of First Nations now live in urban centres (Environics Institute, 2011; FitzMaurice, Kevin, 2012). Indigenous and Northern Affairs Canada (Education and Social Development Programs and Partnerships Sector) manage the Urban Aboriginal Strategy. This programme supports the participation of urban indigenous individuals and communities in the economy, particularly by working to incorporate the crucial role played by urban indigenous organisations across Canada. The Strategy is comprised of two streams: Community Capacity Support; and, Urban Partnerships (INAC, 2015).

Urban Partnerships encourages partnership development and community planning, making investments in projects that increase the participation of urban indigenous people in the economy. This programme brings together governments, indigenous communities and the private and not-for-profit sectors to support projects that remove barriers preventing urban indigenous people from fully participating in the economy. Projects that can be considered for funding include initiatives, research and approaches that increase the economic participation of urban indigenous individuals and communities.

In order to achieve more substantive outcomes in urban indigenous communities, the programme collaborates with key stakeholders to undertake strategic planning, articulate outcomes for communities, identify priorities, and jointly implement initiatives. In its approach, the programme provides a vehicle by which the federal government can work with other governments, urban indigenous organisations, and other stakeholders to support urban indigenous individuals and communities in pursuing social and economic opportunities.

The National Association of Friendship Centres (NAFC) delivers a portion of the Urban Partnerships funding for initiatives that benefit urban indigenous people by responding to priorities identified in the various regional strategic plans developed by INAC in partnership with the provinces and territories.

The Community Capacity Support programme provides operational funding to urban indigenous community organisations to help them maintain a strong and stable base. This strong and stable base enables these organisations to attract further public and private contributions, while assisting them in delivering programs and services on an on-going basis that support the increased participation of urban indigenous people in the economy. The NAFC has been engaged to deliver the Community Capacity Support funding in accordance with programme's objectives and criteria developed by INAC.

Immigrants

The **Immigration, Refugees, and Citizenship** (IRC) Settlement Program assists newcomers outside of Quebec,

The *Canada-Quebec Accord* provides the Government of Quebec with an annual grant, the amount of which is calculated using a formula set out in the Accord. The grant covers settlement services, refugee resettlement and administration for which Quebec is responsible.

to overcome integration barriers so that they can participate in social, cultural, civic and economic life in Canada. Specifically, the Settlement Program aims to help communities build welcoming spaces, as well as provide newcomers with:

- Information about Canada and the community in which they intend to settle.
- The language skills to achieve their settlement and integration goals.
- Assistance in finding and retaining employment.
- The support they need to build networks within their new communities, as well as with employers.

Services are provided pre- and post-arrival through online resources, publications, in-person services as well as through referrals to other available community supports. To address the labour market barriers faced by low and high-skilled newcomers, such as lack of Canadian experience and professional networks, IRC supports a variety of employment services through the Settlement Program, including: the provision of labour market information; employment and job-finding assistance, including Canadian workplace orientation; mentoring and work placements; job-search workshops on networking, resume and interview preparation; job-specific language training; essential skills training; and, preparation for licensure and alternative career initiatives. These services are complemented by services geared towards employers, which help them attract, hire, and retain newcomers.

IRC is continually looking for ways to strengthen its Settlement Program. Currently, the Department is focusing on employment supports for permanent residents, as well as exploring new ways to engage the private sector in welcoming newcomers. IRC partners with nearly 700 organisations, and in some cases, with provincial and territorial programmes, to deliver settlement programming.

In Canada, a license is necessary to perform certain regulated professions and trades, such as doctors, nurses, accountants, lawyers, plumbers, and carpenters. Authorities mandated by each of Canada's ten provinces and three territories provide these licenses. These authorities are responsible to assess and recognise foreign training and experience, also called the Foreign Credential Recognition (FCR) process. The federal government, through the **Foreign Credential Recognition Program** (FCRP), helps licensing authorities, through financial assistance and expertise, to facilitate internationally trained individuals get their credentials recognised so they can put their skills and experience to work faster anywhere in Canada.

A key priority of the FCRP is to implement the 2009 Pan-Canadian Framework for the Assessment and Recognition of Foreign Qualifications (the Framework). The Framework, launched by the Forum of Labour Market Ministers (FLMM), is a joint vision by federal, provincial and territorial governments to work together to ensure that regulatory authorities have FCR processes in place that adhere to the Framework's principles of fairness, consistency, transparency and timeliness. Governments have first targeted 14 in-demand regulated occupations as the common focal point for individual and collective actions: architects, engineers, financial auditors and accountants, medical laboratory technologists, occupational therapists, pharmacists, physiotherapists, registered nurses, dentists, engineering technicians, licensed practical nurses, medical radiation technologists, physicians and teachers. Internationally trained individuals applying to any of these target occupations can expect to have their credentials assessed within one year anywhere in Canada. In 2014 the FLMM announced the addition of 10 new target occupations to the Framework: geoscientists, carpenters, electricians, heavy duty equipment technicians, heavy equipment operations, welders, audiologists and speech language pathologists, midwives, psychologists and lawyers.

FCRP also provides financial support to regulatory bodies and their national professional associations to develop tools and processes with the goal of removing barriers to labour mobility as set out in the amended Chapter 7 of the Agreement on Internal Trade.

In 2012, ESDC launched the Foreign Credential Recognition Loan Pilot. The key goal of the pilot was to determine if there was a need for financial assistance by newcomers for FCR and whether loans would be successful in accelerating the credential recognition process and helping newcomers find commensurate employment. The loans targeted university-educated newcomers intending to work in regulated occupations that are in high-demand in Canada. A successful component of the pilot was the provision of support services by community-based partners to ensure individuals were successful through the credential recognition process, including the development of a career plan and assistance in navigating credential recognition requirements.

Older Workers

The **Targeted Initiative for Older Workers** (TIOW) is a federal provincial/territorial cost-shared initiative designed to support unemployed older workers (normally age 55-64) living in small, vulnerable communities of 250 000 or less which have been affected by high unemployment, significant downsizing/closures, unfulfilled employer demand and/or skills mismatches with their reintegration into employment. Unemployed older workers between the age of 50-54 and over age 64 may also be eligible for TIOW provided that their participation is not at the exclusion of those in the core age group.

Under TIOW, funds are transferred via contribution agreements to provinces and territories based on an allocation. The provinces and territories are responsible for targeting specific communities for interventions as well as for designing and delivering projects that meet their local labour market situations and client needs. Within a TIOW project, a wide range of activity categories are considered eligible, including: basic skills upgrading, specific skills training, community-based work experience, direct marketing to employers and job development and post-project follow-up mentoring and support. employment assistance activities are mandatory for all projects, regardless of other activities. These can include resume writing, interview techniques, informational interviewing, networking, counselling and other related job finding activities.

Vulnerable Persons

Constitutionally, provinces and territories are primarily responsible for social assistance with the exception of specific Government of Canada responsibilities set aside for individuals and families who are ordinarily resident in First Nation reserves (i.e., indigenous peoples). However, the Government of Canada offers funds for a number of programmes designed to assist individuals who have little or no labour force attachment, including those receiving social assistance, to prepare for, obtain and keep employment or to become self-employed.

The **Canada Job Fund Agreements** with provinces and territories provide funding for programming to assist individuals in finding and maintaining employment with priority being given to unemployed persons who are not eligible for EI Part II programming and low-skilled employed. Interventions may include counselling, job search assistance, wage subsidies, on-the-job training, entrepreneurial development, and literacy and basic skills development.

Canadians, particularly from vulnerable groups, may not have the literacy and essential skills needed to fully participate in the labour force. The Office of Literacy and Essential Skills (OLES) works with provincial and territorial governments; postsecondary educational institutions; training service providers; and employers, to help improve the literacy and essential skills of adult Canadians. In particular, the **Adult Learning, Literacy and Essential Skills Program** targets labour market stakeholders as well as groups that are under-represented in the labour force to improve awareness and integration of literacy and essential skills into programmes and activities.

Announced in Budget 2013, the Income Assistance Reform is a horizontal initiative between INAC and ESDC which provides indigenous youth, receiving income assistance, with the skills and training needed to secure employment.

The **Opportunities Fund for Persons with Disabilities** allows persons with disabilities who are unemployed and normally not eligible for EI Part II programming to access a range of interventions and services. These include job search supports, coaching, counselling, resume writing, interview preparation, job placements, tuition assistance, wage subsidies, entrepreneurial training, and employer awareness activities. Starting in 2015-16, this fund will provide more demand-driven training solutions for persons with disabilities and involve employers and community organisations in project design and delivery.

Official Language Minority Communities

The Enabling Fund for Official Language Minority Communities (OLMC) is an integral component of the Government of Canada's strategy for official languages. The federal government is committed to promoting official languages and enhancing the vitality of OLMCs.

ESDC supports this priority through the Enabling Fund, which assists OLMC organisations that employ professional development staff in more than 50 locations across Canada. These organisations constitute a pan-Canadian network of economic and human resource development leaders serving Canada's OLMCs.

EF organisations assist OLMC workers, jobseekers and youth by providing local labour market information and supports to enhance employability. In addition, OLMC organisations develop and broker partnerships with government departments and ministries, and learning and private sector organisations to design/deliver labour market responsive initiatives.

Supporting local economic development in Canada

While there are many organisations and actors involved in economic development activities across Canada, at the federal level, the following departments and organisations have significant activities in Saskatchewan and the Yukon.

Innovation, Science and Economic Development Canada

Innovation, Science and Economic Development Canada is mandated to help make Canadian industry more productive and competitive in the global economy, thus improving the economic and social well-being of Canadians. Competitive businesses are drivers of sustainable economic development. Industry Canada's Small Business Branch is responsible for enhancing growth and competitiveness of small businesses and encouraging entrepreneurship through policy development, and the delivery of programmes. Programmes include the Canada Small Business Financing Program, a loan-loss sharing programme which allows the government to fill a market gap by sharing the risk of lending to small and medium-sized enterprises with financial institutions. Industry Canada's Industrial Research Assistance Program provides innovation and funding services to businesses to help accelerate growth through innovation and technology.

Industry Canada also provides functional guidance to the Business Development Bank of Canada (BDC), which helps to create and develop Canadian businesses through financing, consulting services and securitization, with a focus on small and medium-sized enterprises. BDC also offers specialised financing, including venture capital, equity as well as growth and business transition capital.

Regional Development Agencies work to foster economic development in specific regions of Canada. The six agencies work to support a variety of industry sectors, through targeted business development programmes. They focus on outreach and collaboration efforts that engage local community leaders and stakeholders, including provincial and federal partners, municipalities, indigenous communities, postsecondary institutions, business associations, community economic development organisations, financial institutions, and the not-for-profit sector.

CanNor

The Canadian Northern Economic Development Agency (CanNor) has a mandate to advance economic development in Canada's northern territories and serve as the federal hub for these efforts. It does this by delivering a suite of economic development programmes, aligning the efforts of partners and stakeholders, particularly among federal organisations, and by developing policy and conducting research. As a key element in the "Northern Strategy", the Agency helps to strengthen and diversify the economies in Nunavut, the Northwest Territories and Yukon. CanNor's contribution programmes, which help advance economic development across the territories, include:

- The CAD 40 million (2014-16) Strategic Investments in Northern Economic Development;
- The CAD 10.8 million in annual funding under the Northern Aboriginal Economic Opportunities Program; and
- The five year CAD 27 million Northern Adult Basic Education Program.

Additionally, the agency coordinates and serves as the regional delivery agent for certain national economic initiatives. CanNor's Northern Project Management Office supports responsible northern resource development by providing guidance to industry and communities; coordinating federal efforts related to the regulatory review of major northern projects, and tracking the progress of projects. NPMO supports a more stable and attractive investment climate in the territories by improving the transparency, timeliness and predictability of the environmental assessment and permitting process. Since its creation in 2009, CanNor has invested over CAD 196 million in more than 918 projects in all three territories in key sectors, including mining, geoscience, tourism, fishing, cultural industries, skills development, broadband, power generation and infrastructure.

Western Economic Diversification

A department of the Government of Canada, Western Economic Diversification Canada (WD) was established in 1987 under the provision of the Western Economic Diversification Act. WD works to improve the long-term economic competitiveness of the West (Manitoba, Saskatchewan, Alberta and British Columbia) and the quality of life of its citizens by supporting a wide range of initiatives targeting inter-related project activities to promote innovation, business development, and community economic development.

WD's grants and contributions support projects delivered directly by WD, either alone or in partnership with other organisations. Groups eligible to apply under these programmes include universities and other postsecondary academic institutions, research institutes, industry associations and other not-for-profit organisations. The three main activities are:

- The Western Innovation Initiative offers repayable contributions for small and medium-sized enterprises (SMEs) with operations in Western Canada to move their new and innovative technologies from the later stages of research and development to the marketplace.
- The Western Diversification Program invests in projects that support WD's activities of innovation, business development, community economic development and policy, advocacy and co-ordination, including partnership programmes undertaken with other levels of government.
- The Western Business Service Network is a group of several independent organisations that receive funding from WD to provide a range of services to help create and build small businesses across the West.

References

ESDC (2013), *Aboriginal Labour Market Bulletin*, Volume 2, Issue 2, Employment and Social Development Canada.

Government of Canada (1999), *First Nations Land Management Act*, Ottawa.

Government of Canada (1993), *The Council for Yukon Indians and the Government of the Yukon Umbrella Final Agreement*, Ottawa.

Government of Canada (1985), *Indian Act (R.S.C., 1985, c. I-5)*, Ottawa.

INAC (2015), "First Nations Land Management Regime", Indigenous and Northern Affairs Canada, *www.aadnc-aandc.gc.ca/eng/1327090675492/1327090738973*.

INAC (2013), "Fact Sheet – 2011 National Household Survey Aboriginal Demographics, Educational Attainment and Labour Market Outcomes", Indigenous and Northern Affairs Canada, *www.aadnc-aandc.gc.ca/eng/1376329205785/1376329233875*.

Skof, K. (2011), "Trends in Registered Apprenticeship Training in Canada, 1991 to 2009", *Education Matters: Insights on Education, Learning and Training in Canada*, Vol. 8, No. 3.

Statistics Canada (2015), *Projections of the Aboriginal Population and Households in Canada, Catalogue No. 91-552-X*, ISSN 1927-6389.

Employment and Skills Strategies in Saskatchewan
and the Yukon, Canada

Chapter 3

Saskatchewan's employment and skills system

This chapter provides an overview of key employment and skills policies in Saskatchewan. The Ministry of the Economy plays a key role in the overall management of employment and economic development policies while the Ministry of Advanced Education takes the lead role in the formulation of training and skills programmes. Both ministries work with other provincial level ministries and local delivery organisations to grow the province's economy.

Overview of employment and skills policies in Saskatchewan

Saskatchewan is the middle of the three Prairie Provinces and borders the U.S. to the south. Grassland covers its southern plains, and to the north is the Canadian Shield plateau, as well as coniferous forests, rivers and lakes. Most of its 1.13 million inhabitants live in the southern part of the Province with Saskatoon as the largest city with approximately 257 000 and Regina the province's capital with 210 000. Saskatchewan's population has an annual rate of increase of 1.56% which is among the highest in Canada due largely to inward migration from other provinces and abroad and a high birth rate primarily among Saskatchewan's indigenous population.

Saskatchewan is a comeback story where through the three decades preceding 2006 its population had been shrinking. The last decade has seen the province build a thriving economy that has become a draw for both Canadians and international migrants. Its economy has expanded due to commodity extraction (oil and gas, potash, uranium and metals), agriculture (grains and oil seeds), and services both in the private and public sector.

Local government in Saskatchewan

Saskatchewan's *The Municipalities Act* and *The Cities Act* provide the basic legislative framework for all of the province's southern municipalities. The two Acts also describe the general purpose of municipalities. Section 4(2) of both Acts specify that municipalities have the following purposes:

- To provide good government.
- To provide services, facilities and other things that, in the opinion of council, are necessary or desirable for all or a part of the municipality.
- To develop and maintain a safe and viable community.
- To foster economic, social and environmental well-being.
- To provide wise stewardship of public assets.

Because of the relatively small population base, a number of services that are normally delivered at the municipal level are administered centrally through provincial ministries (in other Canadian provinces, local governments would often provide these services). The most important of these is income assistance but other services such as labour market services are organised and report through the Ministry of the Economy.

While municipalities in Saskatchewan are primarily focused on providing physical services and infrastructure to their residents, local actors are taking an increased interest in labour market activities often in conjunction with the municipalities' interest in economic development. At the same time Ministries responsible for individuals on income assistance recognize that the job market for their clients is local and often dependent on important connections to businesses within the community (Government of Saskatchewan, 2015a).

Ministry of the Economy

The Ministry of the Economy is the lead and primary Ministry responsible for the management of employment and labour market policies; however, both the Ministry of Social Services and the Ministry of Advanced Education play pivotal supporting roles.

The Ministry of the Economy advances economic growth to generate wealth and opportunity in Saskatchewan by attracting investment and removing barriers to growth, facilitating resource exploration and development within an effective regulatory framework; and supporting a robust labour market by developing, attracting and retaining a skilled labour force.

In 2012, the Government of Saskatchewan launched the Saskatchewan Plan for Growth (Government of Saskatchewan, 2012). This is the primary framework through which all labour market and skills policies are developed. The Plan for Growth outlines the provinces direction – principles, goals and actions – to foster economic growth, including the mechanism for development of labour market and skill policies.

The Ministry of the Economy works with other Ministries (e.g. Advanced Education and Social Services) to develop strategies in support of the Plan for Growth. As required, and in relation to specific projects, other Ministries are consulted. For example, the Ministry of the Economy actively participates in a number of forums, including the Advanced Education Technical Trades Planning forum and contributes to integrated, enterprise-wide strategies such as the Poverty Reduction Strategy and the Disability Strategy.

Front line operations are delivered through the Canada-Saskatchewan Labour Market offices that provide career and employment services to job seekers in need of information on career and job opportunities, as well as training and/or education options that enable participation in the provincial labour market as well as services to employers. The services are focused on matching the skills of Saskatchewan workers with the skill needs of employers. Funding assistance to attend training is available under the Skills Training Benefits programme. The Saskjobs website is the provincial job bank that enables employers to post their jobs. On average, there are over 6 500 job vacancies are listed each day. Labour Market Services contracts with community based organisations/third party service providers to provide programming based on regional labour market needs. Programmes are available to help unemployed individuals acquire the fundamental skills they need to participate in the Saskatchewan labour market. Programmes bring together individuals, community-based organisations, employers and government to work in partnership to provide a variety of work preparation opportunities for unemployed people.

A number of targeted programmes are available to help individuals improve their skills to better align with employer job requirements:

- The Targeted Initiative for Older Workers programme, designed to assist unemployed older workers such as (but not limited to) First Nations and Metis peoples with their transition into employment, aligns with the Ministry of the Economy's core lines of business and with the province's Plan for Growth.
- The Canada-Saskatchewan Job Grant is a programme with the intent to "develop the knowledge and skills of Saskatchewan people" by training workers for jobs. The programme is employer driven and has the potential to increase labour market participation of indigenous groups.

- Northern Career Quest is a partnership with federal and provincial governments and northern resource sector companies to support training and employment for indigenous people living in Northern Saskatchewan.
- The Essential Skills for the Workplace programme supports low literacy adults to gain and apply entry-level essential skills within their communities.
- Expanded Adult Basic Education on reserve as well as increased access in urban centres.
- Pilots were initiated in three cities to support First Nations and Métis in their transition from northern or reserve communities into training or jobs in urban centres.

Apprenticeship

Saskatchewan's *Apprenticeship and Trade Certification Act 1999* established the Commission as a Corporation and Agent of the Crown to oversee the provinces apprenticeship system. The Commission reports to the Minister of the Economy and is responsible for designating trades for apprenticeship training and certification; registering apprentices and journey people, monitoring their training and providing certification of skill levels achieved; entering into agreements for training delivery; and representing Saskatchewan on interprovincial initiatives.

A board of 20 or fewer members is appointed by the provincial government, with the majority selected from industry, equally representing employers and employees. The commission board also has representation from Saskatchewan Polytech, the provincial government and equity groups.

Canada-Saskatchewan Job Grant

Recently the Canada-Saskatchewan Job Grant endeavors to put skills training decisions in the hands of Saskatchewan employers and help workers get the training they need for available jobs. Through the grant established in 2014 as a cost shared initiative of the federal government and Saskatchewan, employers partner to fund training for unemployed or underemployed individuals leading to a new or better full-time job. The core principles of the new programme are that the:

- Employer selects the candidates for training and decides what training is required;
- Employer has a job available for the candidate at the end of the training period;
- Employer financially contributes to the training; and
- Training must be provided by an eligible third-party training institution.

To access a Job Grant, an employer is required to contribute at least one third of the training costs, with the remaining two thirds, up to CAD 10 000, coming from the Job Grant. Eligible training costs include tuition fees charged by the training provider, other mandatory student fees, textbook and other learning materials fees, and examination fees.

Ministry of Advanced Education

The Ministry of Advanced Education is responsible for developing a skilled and educated workforce that meets the needs of Saskatchewan's labour market. The Ministry works with the private sector, educational institutions and community organisations to develop, retain, and attract skilled workers. They also work with educational institutions to recruit and retain international students, and assist First Nations and Métis learners. The Ministry works with postsecondary institutions towards system innovation and sustainability (Government of Saskatchewan, 2015b), and to achieve the following goals:

- Increase participation in and completion of high-quality advanced education for all students, especially First Nations and Métis people;
- Retain educated and skilled workers in the province; and,
- Attract students from outside the province and the country by promoting Saskatchewan's opportunities.

Colleges and Universities

Postsecondary programmes and services are delivered through partnerships with a diverse group of institutions and organisations including the University of Saskatchewan in Saskatoon, the University of Regina, First Nations University of Canada in Regina, Saskatchewan Polytechnic, federated and affiliated colleges, regional colleges, Lakeland College, Saskatchewan Indian Institute of Technologies (SIIT), Northern Teacher Education Program/Northern Professional Access College, Dumont Technical Institute (DTI), and Gabriel Dumont Institute (GDI).

The Ministry of Advanced Education engages with the institutions to respond to the needs of the labour market and to ensure accountability of outcomes and effective governance practices. The Ministry provides funding directly to these postsecondary institutions. The Ministry is also responsible for registering and monitoring private vocational schools to ensure compliance with the legislation to protect the interests of their students.

Saskatchewan Polytechnic offers technical and professional programmes with four campuses located in Saskatoon, Regina, Moose Jaw and Prince Albert. A network of seven regional colleges serves smaller communities. For Saskatchewan's indigenous population, there is the Saskatchewan Indian Institute of Technology with Campuses in Saskatoon, Regina and Prince Albert and Gabriel Dumont Institute of Native Studies and Applied Research with campuses in Regina, Saskatoon and Prince Albert (Saskatchewan Indian Institute of Technology, 2014).

Saskatchewan's system is unique in two respects; in the technical and professional studies, planning is done province wide to create a broad offering while keeping the resource commitments to individual programmes reasonable. Saskatchewan Polytechnic, the Regional colleges and the Saskatchewan Indian Institute of Technology collaborate closely jointly offering programmes, sharing resources and not duplicating offerings.

A unique postsecondary institution is the Saskatchewan Indian Institute of Technology (SIIT). Established in 1976 the Saskatchewan Indian Institute of Technologies is a First Nation governed postsecondary institution, recognised under provincial legislation. The Institute grants certificates and diplomas.

SIIT has over 2 000 students into its urban and community programmes as well as serving over 4 800 clients through eight career centres across the province. SIIT is focused on providing work-ready programmes in an indigenous learning environment. Programmes include both in-class and hands-on learning, with close ties to related industry stakeholders to ensure course content is strong and relevant. SIIT provides applied skills training for careers in a variety of areas, including: Adult Basic Education, Business and Information Technology, Community & Health Studies, Professional Development, Trades and Industrial Training.

Ministry of Social Services

The Ministry of Social Services supports vulnerable citizens as they work to build better lives for themselves through economic independence, strong families and strong community organisations. The Ministry assists these efforts with income supports; child and family services; supports for people with disabilities and safe, affordable, accessible housing (Government of Saskatchewan, 2015c).

Targeted Policies and Programmes

Saskatchewan in addition to the range of services for all its citizens provides targeted programmes for a number of groups. Through the Ministry of the Economy, Saskatchewan has 11 Regional Newcomer Gateways that provided co-ordination of services throughout the province. Operating under a settlement service delivery model that integrates such services as:

1. Settlement advisors.
2. ESL language training.
3. Language assessments.
4. Language training – Stage 2 English providing English Training at an intermediate level and English for Employment providing higher language training for the workplace.
5. Immigrant Bridging to Employment (Foreign Qualification Recognition).

Lastly, Saskatchewan has a Provincial Nominee Program, which provides a Saskatchewan Provincial Nomination Certificate to prospective immigrants with the skills and experience targeted by the province to allow them to apply for Canadian permanent residence with processing times that are faster than other Canadian immigration classes.

Indigenous Peoples

For Saskatchewan, First Nations and Métis people are important for the future of the province (Elliot, 2014). The disparity in education and employment outcomes between indigenous and non-indigenous people in Saskatchewan remains one of the province's largest challenges.

While Saskatchewan had one of the lowest unemployment rates among non-Indigenous people in Canada in 2011 (4.6%), the province recorded the second highest indigenous unemployment rate across all the provinces at 16.9% only below the Atlantic region. For on-reserve indigenous in particular, the unemployment rate was 27.7%, compared with 13.4% for indigenous people living off-reserve (Statistics Canada, 2011).

The employment disparity is driven by differences in education outcomes, specifically graduation rates between indigenous and non- indigenous learners. In 2010-11, over 72% of Saskatchewan students graduated "on-time" (within three years of entering grade 10) compared to 32.7% of self-identified indigenous students. The Saskatchewan Ministry of Education also tracks "extended time graduation", recognising that some students require more time to complete Grade 12. The extended time graduation (five years after entering Grade 10) rates were 81.1% for all students and 48.1% for self-identified indigenous students" (Government of Saskatchewan, 2015d).

The province also has a series of goals to:

- Build on the report and recommendations of the Joint Task Force on Aboriginal Education and Employment and seek partnerships with tribal councils, individual First Nations and First Nation businesses to increase employment, businesses and engagement in the economy;

- Reduce the Grade 12 graduation disparity between Aboriginal and non-Aboriginal students in the K-12 system by 50 per cent by 2020; and,
- Work with First Nations partners, employers and postsecondary institutions to build on promising programmes underway that assist in transitioning First Nations students moving off reserve to pursue jobs and educational opportunities.

Saskatchewan has moved away from a single focus point dealing with First Nations and Métis in favour of each Ministry having responsibilities with their mandate to provide services and deal with issues arising from the government's responsibilities for First Nation and Métis. In 2012 the Office of the Provincial Interlocutor for First Nations and Métis Relations was established within Saskatchewan's Ministry of Government to signal the changed nature of the province's vision for its relationship with indigenous people.

The role is to provide a bridge to conversation and engagement between the Saskatchewan government and indigenous organisations – a bridge that also involves and connects non- indigenous stakeholders from across the province. Through its work and the relationships it builds the Office of the Interlocutor promotes the Government's innovation agenda, particularly around shared policy objectives, projects and practical arrangements that improve the outcomes of First Nations and Métis (Government of Saskatchewan, 2014).

References

Elliot, D. (2014), "The Demographic and Economic Characteristics of the Aboriginal Population in Saskatchewan", *Sask Trends Monitor*, Regina, *www.justice.gov.sk.ca/demographic-economic-characteristics-aboriginal-population.*

Government of Saskatchewan (2015a), "Saskatchewan Provincial Budget: Direction for 2015-16", Regina.

Government of Saskatchewan (2015b), "Innovation Saskatchewan Annual Report 2013-14", Regina.

Government of Saskatchewan (2015c), "Ministry of Social Services: Plan for 2015-16", Regina.

Government of Saskatchewan (2015d), "Ministry of Advanced Education: Plan for 2015-16", Regina.

Government of Saskatchewan (2014), "Office of the Provincial Interlocutor for First Nations and Métis Relations – A Bridge to Conversation and Engagement", Regina, *www.embracinglifesk.com/uploads/2/2/8/3/22832950/opi_final_brochure_-_e-copy.pdf.*

Government of Saskatchewan (2012), "Saskatchewan Plan for Growth: Vision 2020 and Beyond", Regina.

Saskatchewan Indian Institute of Technology (2014), "2013-2014 Annual Report".

Statistics Canada (2011), "Aboriginal Peoples in Canada: First Nations People, Métis and Inuit, National Household Survey", *www12.statcan.gc.ca/nhs-enm/2011/as-sa/99-011-x/99-011-x2011001-eng.cfm.*

Employment and Skills Strategies in Saskatchewan
and the Yukon, Canada

Chapter 4

Yukon's employment and skills system

This chapter provides an overview of key actors within the Yukon's employment and skill system. The Department of Education plays a lead role in the development and delivery of employment programmes in the Yukon. Many of the department's recent activities were driven from the conclusion of a Labour Market Framework, which covers a number of important policy areas for employment and economic development.

Overview of Yukon's employment and skills system

The population of Yukon as estimated in June of 2015 was 37 343 in increase of 19.6% (6 121) over the last decade. Whitehorse the capital of the Territory and its largest city had a population of 28 872. Dawson City is the next largest community with a population of 2 067 followed by Watson Lake with 1 469 inhabitants. The remainder of the population is located in 13 smaller communities. Yukon has a large First Nations population of 7 650 as measured in 2014 (YBS, 2015a), representing 20% of Yukon's population.

Local government in Yukon

In the Yukon, municipal governments are formed in accordance with the *Municipal Act* of 2001 and provide services such as water, sewage and waste collection. More recently, municipalities have become more active in fostering local economic development and as a consequence interested in the functioning of the local labour market. Much of the social services for reasons of economy are provided at the Yukon Government level.

Department of Education

On April 1, 2003 a new *Yukon Act* came into effect, giving the Government of Yukon direct control over a greater variety of provincial type programmes, responsibilities and powers. These expanded authorities enabled Yukon to manage its economic future and the ability to respond quickly and effectively to issues as they arose. The Government of Yukon is now responsible for public lands and resource management over water, forestry and mineral resources (Council of Yukon First Nations, 2015a).

Labour Market Services

The Canada-Yukon Labour Market Development Agreement came into force in July 2009 making the government of Yukon responsible for public employment services in the Territory. The Labour Market Programmes and Services Unit (LMPS), Department of Advanced Education, works on strategies and policies to shape Yukon's workforce (Government of Yukon, 2010). The goal of LMPS is to fund Yukon-based persons, organisations and businesses in order that they may acquire the training to grow Yukon's labour force capacity.

The Department of Education has taken a collaborative approach to guide labour market activities for employers and employees through the development of Yukon's Labour Market Framework. The vision of the Labour Market Framework is: an inclusive and adaptable labour market that meets the demands of a strong and diversified economy. The Labour Market Framework has a 10 year horizon: from 2010 to 2020. Five strategies and accompanying priority action plans were developed. The strategies cover:

- Comprehensive Skills and Trades Training;
- Immigration;

- Labour Market Information;
- Recruitment; and Retention.

The Labour Market Framework strategies and action plans were developed in 2009-10 by Working Groups (now referred to as committees) made up of Yukon labour market stakeholders, including business/industry, non-governmental organisations (inclusive of Yukon College), and the federal government and First Nation organisations. While there is crossover and interdependencies between the strategies, each action plan is developed separately by their respective committee.

Each committee meets quarterly and may meet more often as labour market issues are identified. In addition, the chairs of each committee plan additional meetings to address common concerns across the Labour Market Framework's strategies. Many members sit on more than one committee. Members work on a consensus-based decision-making model. Labour Market Framework members take ownership for the development, implementation, monitoring and evaluation of the strategies and action plans.

It is in this context that the Labour Market Information Strategy led to the creation of the Labour Market Information Stakeholder Committee which is co-chaired by Yukon government and stakeholders from the private or non-for-profit sector. This Committee meets on a quarterly basis and on additional occasions when required. The organisations involved on the LMI Stakeholder Committee are: Association Franco-Yukonnaise, Canada-Aboriginal Affairs, Can-Nor, Service Canada, Carpenter Union, Challenge, Employment Central, First Nation of Nacho Nyak-Dun, Multicultural Centre of the Yukon, Northwestel, TIA Yukon, Volunteer Yukon, Whitehorse Chamber of Commerce, Yukon Chamber of Commerce, Yukon College, Yukon Federation of Labour, Yukon Education, Economic Development, Energy, Mines and Resources, Yukon Bureau of Statistics, Public Service Commission, Health and Social Services, Yukon Mining Training Association, and Yukon Worker's Compensation Health and Safety Board.

The LMPS unit of Advanced Education is involved in the management of training and skills development policies, both through the Labour Market Framework and through consultation with other departments and the development of Labour Market Information (LMI). This LMI includes reports compiled by the Yukon Bureau of Statistics, the Government of Canada and other Provinces and Territories with regards to labour market and skills development trends.

An example of LMI influencing training and skills development policies is the 2014 Yukon Training Demand Report. It is a snapshot of in-demand occupations in Yukon for which training is required. Data used to inform the Report comes from the Yukon Bureau of Statistics, Yukon WorkFutures, Statistics Canada and the National Household Survey, and from reports prepared on Yukon Market Supply and Migration. From each source, specific information was extracted to determine population demographics and forecast which occupations will be in high demand for the next three to five years. Such information helps Advanced Education determine applicable training and skills development policies as it relates to setting programme priorities for targeted funding initiatives.

Employment Services

Advanced Education funds Employment Assistance Service (EAS) agencies through the Labour Market Development Agreement. Contract agencies provide job seekers with basic services helping them identify potential job opportunities prepare applications and résumés and prepare for interviews. They may also recommend to Advanced Education individuals who would qualify and benefit from training. Contracts may also be concluded to provide employment services to targeted groups such as disabled Yukoners. Youth are able to use the services offered by the EAS that include resume assistance, job-board postings, and individualized case management.

Targeted services to Youth

Advanced Education also funds the Skookum Jim Friendship Centre (Youth Employment Centre) out of the employment services and supports stream of the Canada Job Fund (Skookum Jim Friendship Centre, not dated). Activities included under this agreement include:

- Job Search – which assists youth (local and in the communities) with job search skills and the job search process. One-on-one services include resume writing, job search strategies, interview preparation and networking. Also funded is the provision of transportation to drop-off resumes and applications and assisting, encouraging and coaching clients to follow-up with employers with regards to their open job postings.
- Wage Subsidy – the provision of a wage subsidy (local and in the communities) to employers to supplement wages, and to encourage the hiring of youth who lack employment experience and may have various employment barriers.
- Job Specific Training – covering the costs for youth to receive short-term job specific pre-hemployment certification such as first aid, food safe, and WHMIS.

Indigenous Peoples

Yukon had at the time of the 2011 NHS 7 700 persons who self-identified as indigenous. This represents 23% of the population of the territory (YBS, 2015b). Yukon has the largest number of self-governing First Nations in Canada (11 of the 17 First Nations in Yukon) and has considerable experience in working on a government to government basis with First Nation communities (Council of Yukon First Nations, 2015b).

The modern-day treaty process began in the Yukon on February 14, 1973, when the Yukon Native Brotherhood, representing 12 Yukon Indian Bands under the leadership of Chief Elijah Smith, presented "Together Today for our Children Tomorrow" to Canada's then Prime Minister Pierre Trudeau. Forty years later, Yukon First Nation self-government is unique in Canada and internationally. The accomplishments of Yukon First Nations are a model for the rest of Canada.

In 2013-2014, the Land Claims and Implementation Secretariat and First Nations Relations amalgamated with the Governance Liaison and Capacity Development Branch into the new Aboriginal Relations Division. This amalgamation provides an enhanced collaborative approach for negotiating and implementing final self-government agreements and other reconciliation arrangements with all Yukon First Nations.

One of the most important functions of the division is organising meetings between Yukon government officials and Yukon First Nation officials and between the Premier and First Nation chiefs. This notion of government-to-government relations is central to how Yukon has structured its interactions with First Nations. Individual departments each have responsibility for dealings with First Nations. As an example First Nation representatives participate on the four working committees of the Labour Market Framework.

Over half of First Nations in the Yukon live in the urban setting of Whitehorse and can access Yukon government services directly. Additionally, First Nations have a Self Government Secretariat (SGS) that was established in 2001 by Council of Yukon First Nations (CYFN) leadership resolution. The purpose of the SGS is to support Self Governing Yukon First Nations (SGYFN) in areas of common concern relating to self-government agreements and includes Yukon First Nations that are not members of the CYFN.

Until 2008, the SGS was overseen by a Chiefs Committee but it now functions as a Self Government Secretariat to the Council of Yukon First Nations. The SGS currently provides support for SGYFN review, renewals and other policy and legislative efforts of common priority to all Yukon Self Governing First Nations. The SGS will continue to assist the Yukon Self Governing First Nations according to the following common objectives:

- Developing governance models, methods and tools to support nation-building;
- Facilitating preparedness of First Nations to negotiate;
- Supporting exploratory and research work as directed by the Self Governing Yukon First Nations, prior to formal negotiations;
- Providing communication and consultation requirements; and
- Supporting development of constitutions, laws and governance structures.

Targeted services to persons with disabilities

Employment needs of persons with disabilities are addressed in the LMF, specifically the CSTTS Action Plan, the first goal of which is "to ensure training opportunities are available for all Yukon people." The following action steps fall within this scope and target persons with disabilities:

- Barriers of participants are identified to improve training delivery methods (1.2.2); and
- Training content is designed to accommodate persons with learning needs (1.2.3).

Funds are managed out of LMPS and all applications are assessed on current programme guidelines, eligible budget categories, available funds and labour market information (Government of Yukon, 2013). Yukon Education and Canada (ESDC) signed the Labour Market Agreement for Persons with Disabilities (LMAPD) on February 19, 2014. The programme went live in August 2014. Under this agreement, Canada will provide CAD 1.25 million annually to Yukon for the next four years, beginning April 1, 2014. Both Yukon Education and the Department of Health and Social Services (HSS) are participating in the administration of the LMAPD. The key principles of the LMAPD in Yukon are the following:

- Provide labour market services to persons with disabilities.
- Eligible participants engaged under this programme must provide informed consent to address an identified or suspected disability.
- The programme is centred on employment-related services provided to participants with a strong focus on case management and participant follow-up.

Yukon Education, in consultation with community stakeholders, developed three streams of programming for persons with disabilities to access labour-market supports. These are:

Capability Assessment & Accommodation Program

This programme supports the activities necessary to assess an individual's workplace capabilities and challenges in order to determine the accommodations necessary for successful engagement with an employer. This requires a broad list of eligible activities to cover the range of assessment tools and strategies, including the creation of individualised assessment strategies, such as a trial work-experience placement with the direct involvement of an occupational therapist. Case management service providers apply for funding to meet the needs of their participants.

Individual Training and Supports Program

This programme is for individuals who need training supports, or individual accommodation supports to gain, maintain or return to employment (such as adaptive technologies or professional supports such as tutoring or counselling).

Workplace Supports Program

This programme allows for a wide range of employment supports including equipment purchase, physical workplace adaptation, tailored job descriptions, job coaching and mentoring, mediation, disability management professionals and wage and earnings subsidies. As with the other programme streams, case management is a key ingredient of the programme. The participant and employer are directly involved in designing the accommodation necessary to achieve the desired result.

The Employment Services and Supports (ESS) stream of the Canada Job Fund supports the Learning Disabilities Association of Yukon (LDAY) which provides services to organisations and professionals who require information and support that will assist them in meeting the needs of adults with learning disabilities. Currently, PSC (Diversity Services) and local NGOs are in the process of creating a Representative Public Service Plan for Persons with Disabilities.

Targeted Initiative for Older Workers

The Targeted Initiative for Older Workers (TIOW) programme helps unemployed workers typically aged 55 to 64, return to work. The initiative is cost-shared with the Canadian provinces and territories. It provides employment assistance services, such as resume writing and counselling, and improves participants' employability through activities such as skills upgrading and work experience.

Through a TIOW funding agreement between Yukon government and Employment and Social Development Canada, Yukon Education administers funding to Yukon College to deliver the Yukon TIOW programme. The programme is delivered at Yukon College's Whitehorse campus.

Over the period 1 April 2014 to 31 March 2017, Yukon College will deliver the TIOW programme to approximately 72 older workers through a 15-week course that includes a four-week job placement offered in Fall and Spring. This funding has been in place since 2006 and it has continually gained in popularity over the years for Yukon's older workers. Participants while enrolled in the programme are eligible to receive an hourly stipend equal to Yukon's minimum wage which does not contravene their Employment Insurance benefits. Reports indicate positive employment outcomes with over 75% of participants gaining employment at course completion.

Policies and programmes for immigrants

The Education Department is responsible for immigration the Yukon as immigration is seen in a broader labour market context. The single goal of the immigration strategy is to support a responsive and sustainable approach to Yukon immigration (Government of Yukon, 2010b). This goal is supported by the following six objectives:

- Be responsive to industry and business labour force needs through the improvement and monitoring of the Yukon nominee programme;
- Assist more immigrants to engage in Yukon's labour market opportunities by providing better information and services;
- Ensure the provision of settlement services is inclusive for all newcomers, including temporary foreign workers and Yukon nominee program participants;
- Provide immigrants with the resources and training they need to seek further education to work in their chosen field or to access better employment opportunities;
- Support immigrant communities within Yukon by helping them to increase their capacity, their profile and the services they offer their membership; and
- Increase immigrant retention rates by promoting the benefits of immigration and celebrating multiculturalism.

The Yukon Nominee Program is part of the Yukon Immigration Strategy. The Yukon Nominee Program (YNP) is run by the Yukon Government in partnership with Citizenship and Immigration Canada under the "Agreement for Canada-Yukon Cooperation on Immigration". This partnership allows Yukon to nominate applicants who qualify to the federal government for permanent residency.

The YNP streams for Skilled Workers and Critical Impact Workers is locally driven and based on the needs of Yukon employers. When eligible Yukon employers cannot find Canadian citizens or permanent residents to fill permanent full-time jobs, they can find workers from outside of Canada. The YNP also includes Express Entry and Yukon Business Nominee streams.

A strategic approach to immigration helps the Yukon government respond to labour market needs in a way that can be sustained through fluctuating economies while ensuring that job opportunities are safeguarded for Yukoners and Canadians.

Economic Development

The Department of Economic Development is involved in the management of economic development policies. The mandate of this department is to develop a sustainable and competitive Yukon economy to enrich the quality of life of all Yukoners; to pursue economic initiatives with a shared vision of prosperity, partnerships and innovation; and to forge partnerships with First Nations in the economic development of the territory (Government of Yukon, 2012). The primary responsibilities of the Department of Economic Development are to:

- Develop and maintain a sustainable and competitive Yukon economy to enrich the quality of life of all Yukoners;
- Pursue economic initiatives with a shared vision of prosperity, partnership and innovation;
- Forge, maintain and expand partnerships with First Nations in the economic development of Yukon;

- Work in partnership with First Nations and others initiating or implementing regional economic plans;
- Proactively administer the Community Development Fund.

Activities of the Department are informed by "Pathways to Prosperity" that sets the economic vision for Yukon through 2025. The broad vision in Pathways is "Strategically situated, with shipping access to Asian markets and providing a land link between Alaska and the rest of North America, Yukon is positioned to leverage its advantages of world class mineral and oil and gas deposits, breathtaking scenery, and skilled and adaptable people." The strategy looks at three components: wealth generators including mines, tourism, the film industry and exports from value-added activities; support industries such as transportation, retail and professional services will expand to service the wealth generators and support the needs of a growing population; and, enabling factors such as research and innovation, policy and regulations, infrastructure, capacity development and business promotion and facilitation.

References

Council of Yukon First Nations (2015a), "History of land Claims", *http://cyfn.ca/history/history-of-land-claims/.*

Council of Yukon First Nations (2015b), *First Nations Education Commission (FNEC), http://cyfn.ca/services/education/first-nations-education-commission/.*

Government of Yukon (2013), "Yukon First Nations Funding Sources", Whitehorse, *www.eco.gov.yk.ca/pdf/web_Yukon_First_Nation_funding_sources_2013Final.pdf.*

Government of Yukon (2012), "Department of Economic Development Strategic Plan 2012-17", Whitehorse, *www.economicdevelopment.gov.yk.ca/pdf/EcDev_Strat_Plan_2012-2017.pdf.*

Government of Yukon (2010a), "Labour Market Framework Strategies: Comprehensive Skills and Trades Training Strategy Action Plan", Whitehorse, *www.labourmarketframeworkyukon.com/system/PDF/LMI%20strategy.pdf.*

Government of Yukon (2010b), "Labour Market Framework for Yukon: Immigration Strategy", Whitehorse, *http://labourmarketframeworkyukon.com/system/PDF/labour_market_framework-web.pdf.*

YSB (2015a), "Yukon Fact Sheet June 2015", Yukon Bureau of Statistics, Whitehorse, *www.eco.gov.yk.ca/pdf/Web_Factsheet_Jun_2015.pdf.*

YBS (2015b), "Yukon Employment Annual Review 2014", Yukon Bureau of Statistics, Whitehorse, *www.eco.gov.yk.ca/pdf/employment_2014.pdf.*

Yukon First Nations (2014), "Yukon First Nations (YFN) Joint Education Action Plan: 2014-2024", *http://cyfn.ca/wp-content/uploads/2013/09/Approved-JEAP.pdf.*

Employment and Skills Strategies in Saskatchewan
and the Yukon, Canada

Chapter 5

Overview of the case study areas in Saskatchewan and Yukon

This chapter provides a labour market and economic overview of the four case study regions as well as a description of their employment and training services. It also presents the results from an OECD LEED statistical tool which looks at the relationship between skills supply and demand at the sub-national level. To better understand the role of the local level in contributing to job creation and productivity, this study examines local activities in four case study areas across Saskatchewan and Yukon: 1) Whitecap Dakota First Nation; 2) Regina; 3) Whitehorse; and 4) Dawson City.

Overview

In-depth fieldwork for this study was undertaken in four areas across Saskatchewan and Yukon. These areas were selected after consultation between the OECD and a steering group of federal and provincial and territorial government representatives. In Saskatchewan, the study examined local activities in Whitecap and Regina. In the Yukon, local activities were examined in the municipalities of Whitehorse and Dawson City. This chapter begins by giving a labour market and economic overview of the four case study areas as well as a description of the employment and training services that are available in each. This is followed by the results of a statistic tool developed by the OECD LEED Programme, which looks at the relationship between supply and demand for skills at the sub-national level.

Whitecap Dakota First Nation, Saskatchewan

Whitecap is a small community located 26 kilometres south of Saskatoon (Whitecap Dakota First Nation, 2015). Formerly known as Moose Woods, it was established in 1889 by Order-in-Council. The Whitecap Dakota First Nation is part of the larger Dakota Nation, whose traditional governance structure was called the Seven Council Fires or Oceti Sakowin, and whose traditional lands extended into both Canada and the United States. The reserve occupies 19.29 square kms. According to the 2011 NHS, the population within this community was 350, an increase of 48.9% from 2006. The increase is related to a number of economic development activities that have greatly increased employment opportunities in the community. The total Band membership is 629 as of 2015, not all of which are residing on reserve (City of Saskatoon, 2015).

Economic activity

Whitecap has been successful at launching a number of enterprises. The largest is the Dakota Dunes Casino and Resort, a joint venture with the Saskatoon Tribal Council which employs over 400 people. The Dakota Dunes Golf Club adjacent to the Casino is recognised as one of Canada's top 10 golf courses. A gas station and convenience store called Whitecap Trail Gas Plus brings in over CAD 1 million per year and creates additional employment. There are approximately 700 full time, part time, and seasonal jobs in Whitecap (Anderson, 2014).

The Whitecap Development Corporation has several partnerships that are beginning to bring industrial activity to the area (The Canadian Business Journal, 2011). Whitecap Commercial Real Estate develops unique commercial and light industrial properties both on and off Whitecap Dakota Lands. A 15 000 square foot storage building has been constructed and is the first development in the Whitecap Trail Business Park. The park will provide fully serviced land to attract light industrial businesses. The storage is currently fully leased. Whitecap Industrial Services is a partnership comprised of some of the most respected service providers in the resource industry. It is the newest division of the Whitecap Development Corporation and is focused on providing diverse and complementary services to the mining, oil & gas, pipeline, and utilities industries in Saskatchewan. The Tatanka Bison

Ranch manages a herd of bison and grazing lands for future expansion. Raising bison for breeding stock and meat has historical significance for the Whitecap Dakota First Nation.

Much of the economic activity is driven by land reform. Whitecap Dakota First Nation created its own land code in 2004 and is currently under the federal government's First Nation Land Management Act. This has eliminated 25% of provisions from the Indian Act and has given Whitecap government control over the management of Whitecap's land and resources. A second generation Land Code was implemented in 2010 in consultation with financial institutions and Canada Mortgage and Housing Corporation which further enhance the investment and security environment for lenders.

The Whitecap Dakota First Nation developed a Land Use Plan that divided the reserve into Land Use Zones with each zone having its own development standards to maximise land values. Forty-nine (49) year commercial and 99 year residential leasing instruments with renewal options give the band the flexibility to meet the needs of inward investors.

Business development legislation including property taxation, business licensing, environmental management along with a CAD 12 million infrastructure investment was made to support commercial and residential development. This has helped to raise the market value of Whitecap Lands and create employment opportunities.

Figure 5.1. **Map of Saskatoon, Saskatchewan and Whitecap Dakota First Nation**

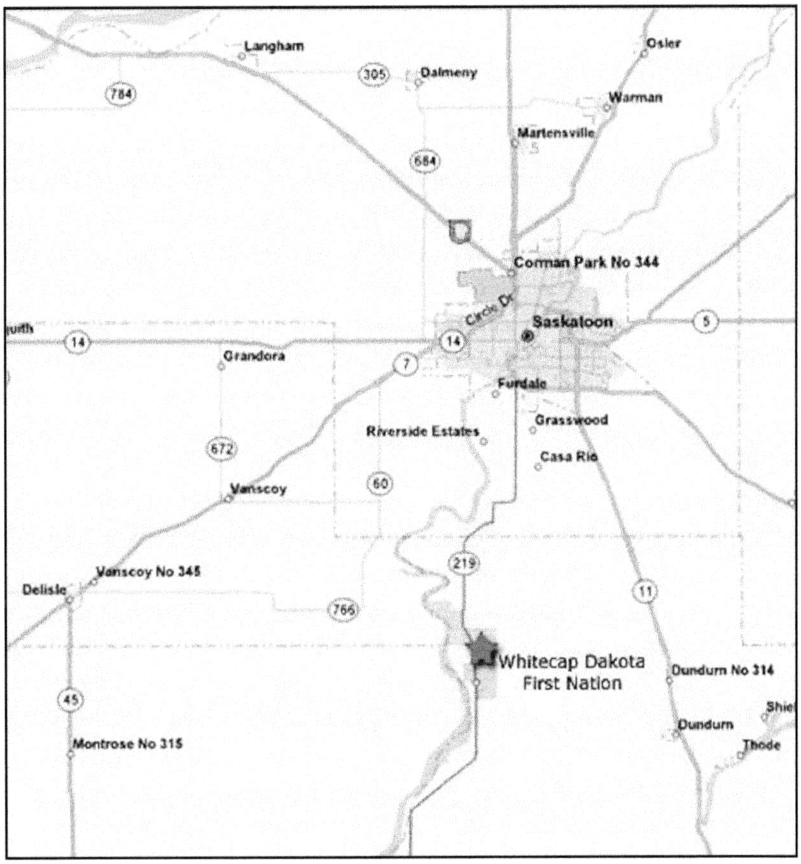

Source: Whitecap Dakota First Nation, about us, available at *www.whitecapdakota.com/about/location-maps/.*

Education

The Whitecap Dakota First Nation has K4 to grade four programmes in the community. From Grade 5, students go to Saskatoon for their studies. What is significant about Whitecap is that its school is part of the Saskatoon Public School Division. To support this arrangement, Indigenous and Northern Affairs Canada funded the Saskatoon Public School Division in accordance with the Saskatchewan Ministry of Education funding formula. As before, once students have completed high school, they may attend Saskatchewan Polytechnic, SIIT or University of Saskatchewan in Saskatoon or any number of other postsecondary institutions in the Province or in other jurisdictions. The high school graduation rate is about the same as that for non-indigenous students and considerably higher than the provincial average for First Nations (Government of Yukon, 2015a).

Employment and income assistance

Employment services are provided by the band administration for members of the community. Employment opportunities abound and in fact about 100 people commute from Saskatoon to jobs in Whitecap (Anderson, 2014). The Saskatoon Tribal Council provides members who have moved to Saskatoon employment services.

In 2014-15, there were a total of 82 Income Assistance beneficiaries in the community (30 children aged 0-17 and 52 adults). This number represents approximately 23% of the population of the community. These services are provided through the band administration.

Regina, Saskatchewan

Regina is the second most populous municipality in Saskatchewan and the Province's capital. In 2011 the Census Metropolitan Area (CMA) of Regina recorded a population of 210 556 having grown 8.0% in the previous 5 years (the average growth rate among CMAs is 7.4%). The census recorded 85 731 private dwellings in Regina an increase of 6.7% over 2006 but lower that the average increases in CMAs which was 7.1%. In recent years the population has continued to grow reaching 232 090 in 2014. Immigration appears to make up 65% of the recent increase with natural growth representing 18%. Eleven percent of the increase is intra-provincial migration with a significant portion of those flows coming from indigenous people moving from reserves to the city (Hemson Consulting Ltd, 2013).

Economic activity

The Economy of Regina is driven by the public sector; as the capital, the city has many of the provinces Ministries and a significant public sector workforce (Regina Regional Opportunities Commission, 2015). Private companies have in recent decades played a more important role and sectors such as agriculture, mining, and oil extraction are well represented in the city. Newer industries such as logistics, metal fabrication and advanced manufacturing are finding a stronger place in the economic fabric of Regina and it is expected that a strong private sector will continue to propel the City's growth in the future. The Regina economic region extends well beyond the boundaries of the city of Regina. Production networks connect the potash mines, oil fields and agricultural production in areas far from Regina with the services that are found within the city, such as construction; research and development; marketing, finance and legal services; logistics and technical support.

A good example of the City's innovation in development is the Global Transportation Hub, Canada's only autonomous and self-governing Inland Port Authority. The Global Transportation Hub is located beside the Canadian Pacific (CP) railway mainline and between two national highway system routes providing direct access to all major Canadian ports, gulf coast ports, and mid-western US ports, as well as trucking connections to all major markets including Trans-Canada, Minneapolis, Chicago, and Mexico.

Figure 5.2. **Map of Regina, Saskatchewan**

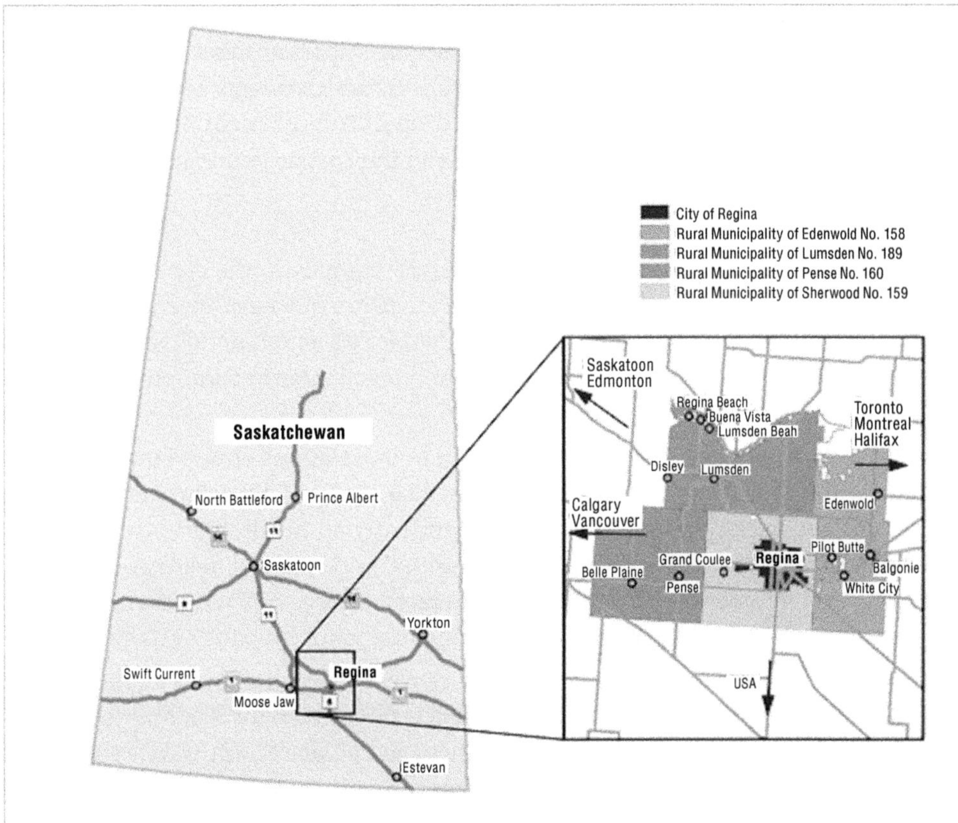

Source: Government of Saskatchewan.

Regina's local economic and employment development services

The Regina Regional Opportunities Commission (RROC) is the agency responsible for advancing economic development and tourism in the Regina region. RROC provides leadership to the community with specific accountability for the following core functions:

- Support industry growth and diversification through retention, development and attraction of industry and tourism;
- Find innovative ways to promote sustainable growth while effectively addressing the challenges of associated with it;
- Market and promote the Regina region for business and tourism;
- Ensure the Regina region offers a vibrant and diversified economy for investors, is a positive destination experience for visitors and offers a high quality of life for residents.

RROC has been looking at how Regina can develop sector ecosystems in manufacturing, metal fabrication, agri-business and tourism. The Regina Chamber of Commerce is active in all areas of Regina's development. The Chamber plays an active role in promoting the city as a great place to do business and live. It is also active in labour market development through participation in the Regina Skills and Trades Centre and in other activities for skills development.

The Regina campus of SOCO opened in 2000. Located next to the University of Regina, Innovation Place hosts leading edge petroleum, environmental sciences and information technology organisations. Innovation Place is home to 27 tenants, employing over 1 300 people. The park includes 6 buildings with 465 000 square feet of space. The Regina Campus is part of one of three campuses operated by Saskatchewan Opportunities Corporation (SOCO). SOCO supports the advancement and success of Saskatchewan's technology and key growth sectors through the development and operation of technology parks at the province's universities in Saskatoon and Regina and the Forest Centre in Prince Albert.

Education and vocational training in Regina

The University of Regina is the largest university campus in the city with over 14 000 full-time and part-time students. Major fields of study are business, science, engineering, nursing and arts. The University of Regina is known for its experiential learning approach and offers internships, professional placements and practicums in addition to co-operative education placements in 41 programmes.

In May 1976, the Federation of Saskatchewan Indian Nations entered into a federation agreement with the University of Regina, to establish the Saskatchewan Indian Federated College. The Agreement provided for an independently administered university-college, the mission of which is to serve the academic, cultural and spiritual needs of First Nations' students. In 2003, the Saskatchewan Indian Federated College officially changed its name to the First Nations University of Canada. Annual enrollment is about 3 000 students.

The university offers programmes and services on three campuses: Regina, Saskatoon and Prince Albert (Northern Campus). Since 1983, the university has entered into over 25 agreements with indigenous peoples' institutions in Canada, South and Central America and Asia and signed academic exchange agreements with institutions in Siberia (Russia), Inner Mongolia (China) and Tanzania.

Saskatchewan Polytechnic has a large campus in Regina with programmes offered in ten schools focusing on: animal and bio-sciences, business; construction; health sciences; hospitality and tourism; mining, energy and manufacturing; transportation; nursing; information and communication technologies; and, human services and community safety. Saskatchewan Polytechnic offers degrees, diplomas and certificates. The Polytechnic provides the in-school portion of apprenticeship training for 20 trades. Saskatchewan Apprenticeship and Trade Certification Commission (SATCC) schedules the apprenticeship training.

The Regina Trades and Skills Centre was established as a not-for-profit with the goal of delivering short-term trades and skills training that leads to entry-level jobs in industries where workers are in high demand. The Centre works with industry to develop and deliver relevant and recognised programmes that are responsive to industry needs for trained and skilled workers.

Employment Services

The Ministry of Economy labour market services has one location in central Regina. The office receives job seekers and provides basic services such as access to job postings, work stations to complete resumes, and limited counselling to anyone looking for work. For those who qualify under Employment Insurance or are in receipt of income assistance and part of the "T-program" additional counselling and testing services are available as well as the possibility of training. Labour Market Services contracts with providers that deal with special needs clients and for the provision of job readiness services. Contracts are awarded based on the Labour Market Services' appreciation of client demand and the past performance of contracted agencies.

Income Assistance

While the Ministry of Social Services administers income assistance at a provincial level those individuals who are judged to be capable of working are referred to Labour Market Services for counselling, training and job placement assistance. A number of contracts have been established with agencies to provide job readiness training, many of whom will organise job placements.

Whitehorse, Yukon

Whitehorse is the capital of Yukon and the Territory's largest city. The 2011 census reported 26 028 usual residents in the Whitehorse Census Metropolitan Area an increase of 13.9% from the 2006 census. Population growth in Whitehorse has been faster than Canada and the Yukon Bureau of Statistics estimates Whitehorse's current population at 28 872 (June 2015) or 77% of the population of the Yukon. While small by the standards of Canada's southern cities, Whitehorse has amenities and infrastructure similar to a larger municipality (City of Whitehorse, 2015).

Figure 5.3. **Map of Yukon, showing Whitehorse and Dawson City**

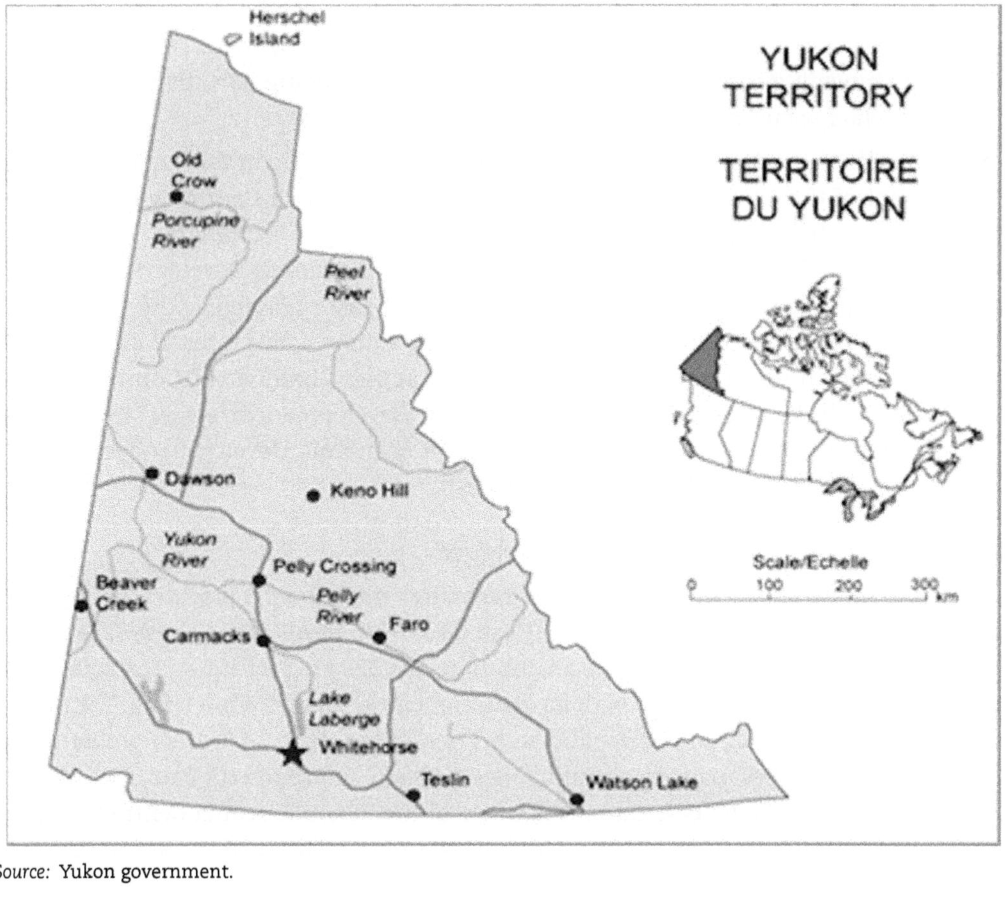

Source: Yukon government.

Whitehorse's local economic and employment development services

The local economy of Whitehorse is dominated by the public service with about 34% of the work force reporting that they worked in public administration or health and social services in the 2011 National Household Survey. Tourism is the next largest generator of employment with 7% of the workforce in the accommodation and food services industry. Nearly 13% of workers reported working in retail trades and 9% in construction (Government of Yukon, 2015b; YBS, 2013).

There are two First Nations communities that have traditional lands within the municipal boundaries of Whitehorse Kwanlin Dün and Ta'an Kwäch'än. Both are self-governing. Kwalin Dün, the largest of Yukon's First Nations, finalised its self-government agreement in 2005 that awarded it control over 1 042 km^2 of which 30km^2 is in the municipal boundary of Whitehorse. Under its land claim, the Ta'an Kwäch'än traditional territory covers approximately 12 079 km^2, of which 796 km^2 are designated as settlement lands. Over 50% of the Ta'an people live in Whitehorse.

Employment Central, an agency contracted by the Department of Education, provides basic services to all jobseekers. Those looking for work have access to a job board, workstations to prepare resumes and some counseling from staff. Qualified EI claimants may be eligible for training and these clients receive more intensive case management services. Specialised job search services are provided for persons with disability and for youth by other agencies under contract.

Both Kwalin Dün and Ta'an Kwäch'än have employment counselors funded through the ASETs programme that provide support for job seekers in those First Nation communities. The Department of Health and Social Services has recently expanded services to assist individuals on income assistance to find employment. These services, in addition to providing case support to job seekers, are expanding its activities to contact employers who may be interested in providing clients with work.

Much of the economic development of Whitehorse is tied up in the overall economic development of the Territory. Facilities like the Yukon Research Centre, while targeting activities across the Territory, bring researchers and funding to Whitehorse. In the spring of 2015, the City of Whitehorse developed a Community Economic Development Strategy that laid the base for a series of activities designed to boost economic activity in the city over the next 5 years. This will involve the city taking a more active interest in and role in building the local economy. Whitehorse has an active Chamber of Commerce that participated with the City to complete the Economic Development strategy. The Chamber also offered programmes and worked with Yukon Economic Development to promote entrepreneurship and small business development.

Education and vocational training in Whitehorse

Yukon College is the Territory's only postsecondary institution. It provides a wide range of programmes focused on the employment and leadership needs of the North. The college has about 1 200 students (of which 681 are full-time and 526 are part-time). The college has 13 campuses located across Yukon with its main campus located in Whitehorse. The college offers a variety of academic and vocational programming, such as: access programmes; career and job readiness; part-time continuing education courses; certificate; diploma and degree courses. The Whitehorse campus is home to the Yukon Research Centre (YRC), the Centre for Northern Innovation in Mining and the Northern Institute of Social Justice.

Dawson City

Dawson City is situated 435 km north and west of Whitehorse. It was the original capital of the Territory and for the short period around the 1898 gold rush was the largest community west of Winnipeg and north of Seattle. The population in 1898 was over 40 000 while recently, it is estimated to be over 1 300 (1 319 reported in the 2011 census). The population of the town was stable between 2006 and 2011. Dawson City demographic trends show an aging population with growing numbers in the senior groups over 54 years. About 30% of Dawson city's residents identify as indigenous, 12.5% as French speaking. Of the non-indigenous population, over 50% indicate that they were born outside of Yukon.

Dawson City's local economic and employment development services

Dawson City's labour force is reported to be 1 115 with an overall participation rate of 83.9%. The employment rate is 72.6% and unemployment sits at 13.4%. It is worth noting that a significant difference between the male and female unemployment rates exists (males at 16.5% and females at 9.5%).

The main employers in Dawson City are governments (federal, territorial, First Nation and municipal). Tourism plays a significant role in the employment sector in the services industry, along with employment opportunities in placer and hard rock mining. Tourism and mining tend to be seasonal by nature and a large number of seasonal workers relocate to Dawson City during the summer months. The retail trade and construction industry benefit from these main industries (Klondike Development Organization, 2013).

Klondike Outreach, an agency contracted by the Yukon Department of Education, provides employment services. Basic Services are provided to all job seekers, with more intensive services provided to those who qualify for EI. Two areas of preoccupation for the employment services are the large volume of seasonal workers who come to Dawson City during the summer to work in the hospitality and mining industries and a growing cadre of older seasonal workers who can no longer work under the demanding conditions of their profession but possess few skills readily transferable to other forms of employment.

The people of Dawson City are adaptable, creative, entrepreneurial and innovative. The City has recognised its need to offer strong leadership to ensure its future prospects. Much of the energy is being placed in the area of tourism with a major initiative to have the town that contains 8 Parks Canada historic sites and numerous other artefacts dating from the Klondike Gold Rush as a UNESCO World Heritage Site. Another feature of Dawson City is the close working relationship between the First Nation government of Tr'ondëk Hwëch'in and the Municipal Government. In fact it is the Tr'ondëk Hwëch'in administration that is doing much of the work to prepare the UNESCO application.

A self-organised group of some of Dawson's leading business and community leaders formed a partnership between the City of Dawson, Dawson City Chamber of Commerce, Klondike Visitors Association, Dawson City Arts Society and Chief Isaac Inc. to create Klondike Development Organization in 2009. The Regional Economic Development initiatives are now led by the North Yukon Regional Economic Action Development Initiative (READI). Tr'ondëk Hwëch'in administers READI with co-funding from the Government of Yukon and the City of Dawson.

Education and vocational training in Dawson City

Dawson City has a campus of Yukon College that provides young people with postsecondary programmes that can be completed in Whitehorse and professional development course to build local business capability. Yukon School of Visual Arts (SOVA) is a postsecondary art school located in Dawson City. SOVA is part of the Applied Arts Division of Yukon College, and receives its academic accreditation through the College.

Attracting and certifying apprentices has proved challenging for Dawson City. Tr'ondëk Hwëch'in has initiated an innovative approach in registering apprentices through the First Nation administration (Tr'ondëk Hwëch'in Council, 2014). This allows the apprentice to work for several employers completing different requirements of the apprenticeship while maintaining the work log in one place. This facilitates the experience for both the apprentice and the small business owners.

Provincial profiles for Saskatchewan and Yukon

Population

According to the 2011 National Household Survey, there were just over 1 million people living in Saskatchewan and around 33 000 people living in the Yukon territory. More recent data show that between 2005 and 2015, the population of Saskatchewan and Yukon grew by 14% and 12% respectively (Saskatchewan Bureau of Statistics, 2015a; YSB, 2015a). In 2011, the population of Saskatchewan was younger than that of Yukon, with 33.5% of the population aged less than 25 compared to 30.7%.

The share of people identifying themselves as indigenous is 15.3% in Saskatchewan and 23.1% in Yukon, which is significantly higher than the national average of 4.3%. Figure 5.4 shows the proportion of First Nations, Métis and Inuit among the population in the two provinces and in Canada.

In 2011, the indigenous population was younger than the non-indigenous population in both Saskatchewan and Yukon, with 53.7% of indigenous people in Saskatchewan and 42.5% in Yukon being aged less than 25 (29.8% and 27.2% in the non-indigenous population respectively).

Educational attainment

Figure 6.5 shows the gap that exists in terms of educational attainment between indigenous and non-indigenous populations aged 15 or more in Yukon, Saskatchewan and Canada as a whole. When looking at the share of individuals holding a postsecondary certificate, diploma or degree, this gap is wider in Yukon (22.6%) and in Saskatchewan (18.5%) than in Canada as a whole (16.8%). The same is true for individuals holding no certificate, diploma or degree.

Labour market

As figure 5.6 shows, in 2011, overall labour market participation and employment rates are higher in the Yukon and Saskatchewan when comparing the non-indigenous population to the rest of Canada. However, when looking at the indigenous population, one can see that both their participation and employment rates are well below the non-indigenous population. This holds in both the Yukon and Saskatchewan as well as when looking at the average of Canada.

Figure 5.4. **Share of indigenous population by Indigenous groups (First nations, Métis, Inuit), 2011**

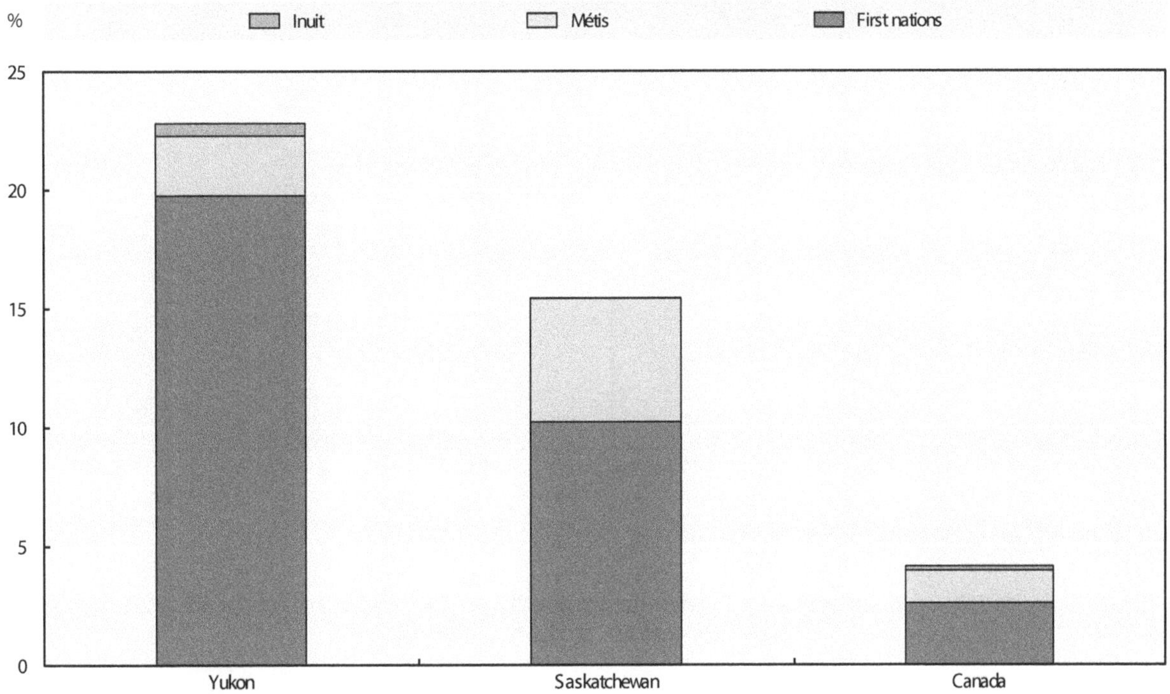

Source: Statistics Canada, 2011 National Household Survey.

Figure 5.5. **Highest Certificate, Diploma or Degree, Population aged 15 years or more by Indigenous identity, Canada, Yukon, Saskatchewan, 2011**

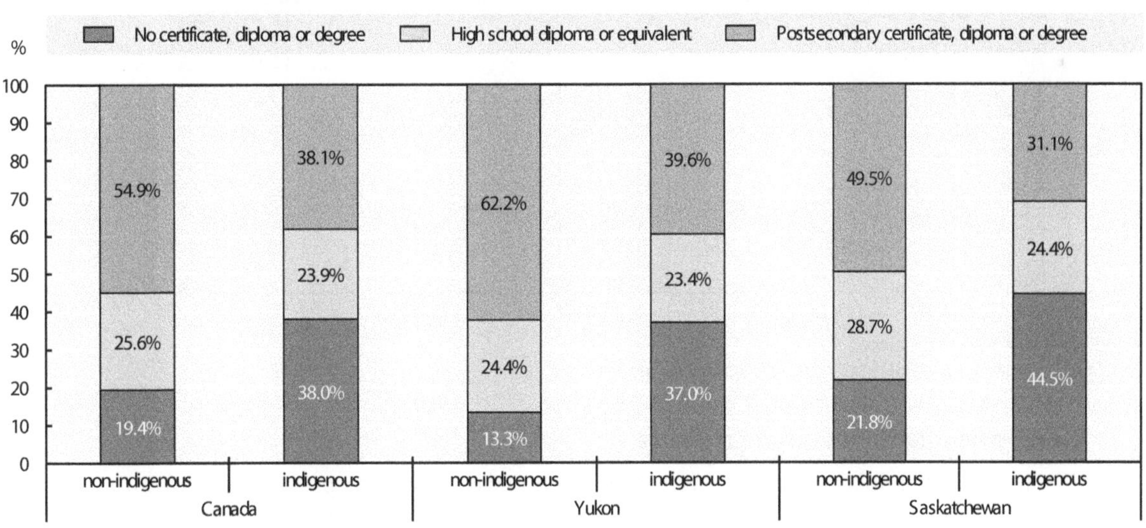

Source: Statistics Canada, 2011 National Household Survey.

While youth unemployment increased in Canada as a whole between 2006-14 from 11.6% to 13.5%, it declined both in Saskatchewan and Yukon (see Figure 5.7), showing that these provinces were probably less impacted by the recent crisis.

Figure 5.6. **Participation and employment rates, Population aged 15 years or more, Yukon, Saskatchewan, Canada average, 2011**

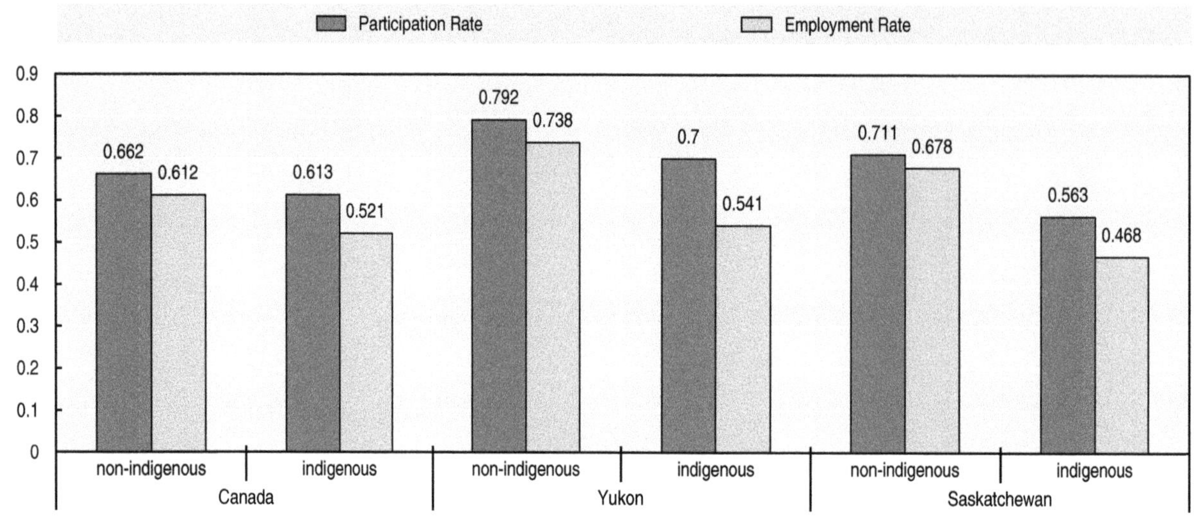

Source: Statistics Canada, 2011 National Household Survey.

Figure 5.7. **Youth unemployment, Population aged 15 to 24,* Canada (excluding territories), Saskatchewan, Yukon, 2006-14**

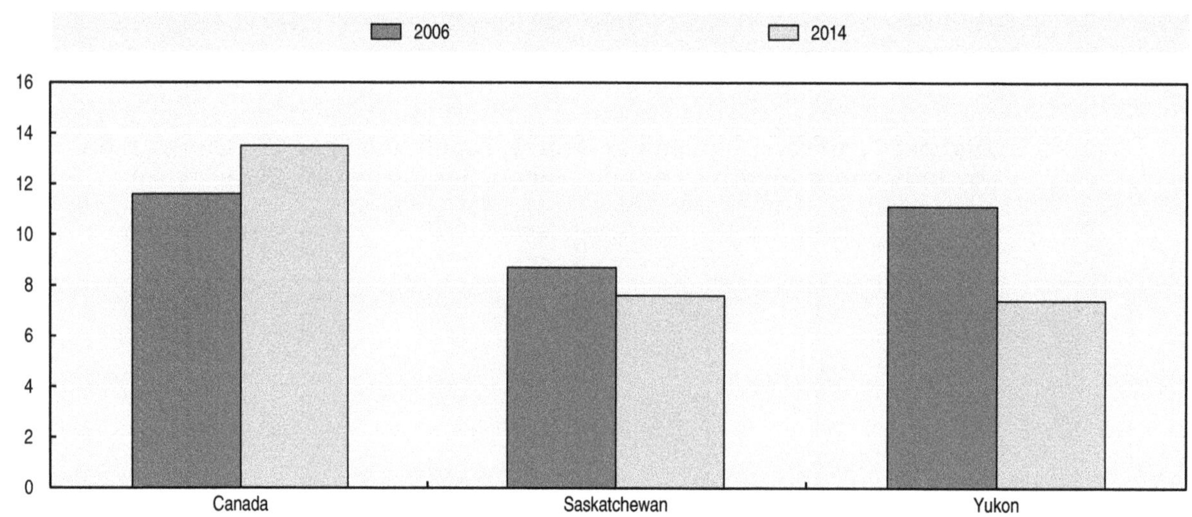

* Excluding people living on-reserve.
Source: Statistics Canada, CANSIM table 282-0087, Labour Force Survey.

Employment and industrial structure

In 2014, the labour market structure of the two provinces presented a number of differences (Saskatchewan Bureau of Statistics, 2015b; YSB, 2015b). In terms of employment by sector, Yukon was characterised by high shares of employment in public administration, followed by trade and health care and social assistance, whereas in Saskatchewan employment was more concentrated in trade, health care and social assistance and construction (Figure 5.8).

Both Yukon and Saskatchewan had a higher proportion of workers registered as self-employed than the Canadian average (15.3%) at 16.5% and 19.4% respectively. As shown in

Figure 5.8. **Share of employment by select industry categories, population aged 15 years or more,* Saskatchewan, Yukon, 2014**

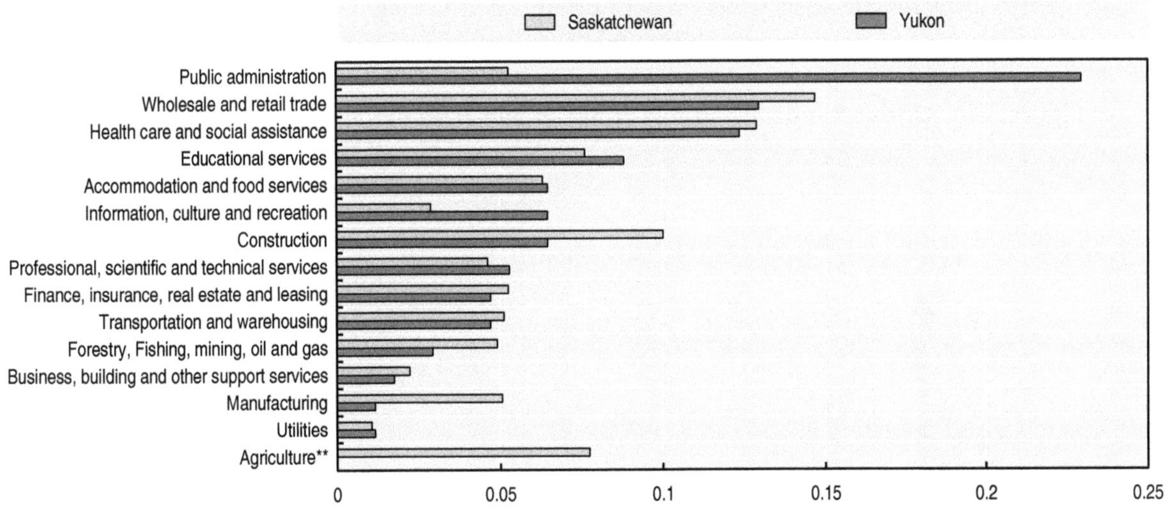

* Excluding people living on-reserve.
** Data not available for Yukon.
Source: Statistics Canada, CANSIM table 282-0012, Labour Force Survey; YSB (2015a).

Figure 5.9, in both Saskatchewan and Yukon, sales and service occupations account for the largest share of employment. Saskatchewan has a much higher share of employment in occupations unique to primary industries due to the importance of the extractive industries in the Province.

Figure 5.9. **Share of employment by occupations, Population aged 15 years or more,* Saskatchewan, Yukon, 2014**

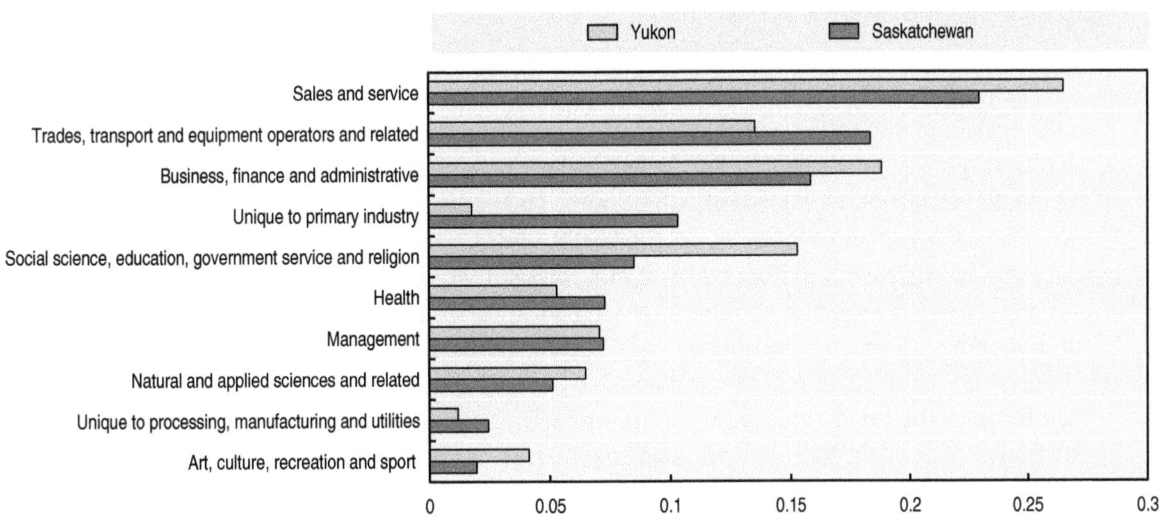

* Excluding people living on-reserve.
Source: Statistics Canada. Table 282-0232 – Labour force survey estimates (LFS).

Labour force dynamics

To supplement the above analysis, the OECD LEED Programme has developed a statistical tool to understand the balance between skills supply and demand within local labour markets (Froy, Giguère and Meghnagi, 2012). In the Canadian context, this tool can supplement the previous analysis to provide policy makers with an understanding of potential skills mismatches, which may be occurring at the sub-national level. It can also inform place-based policy approaches at the local level.

Figure 5.10. **Understanding the relationship between skills supply and demand**

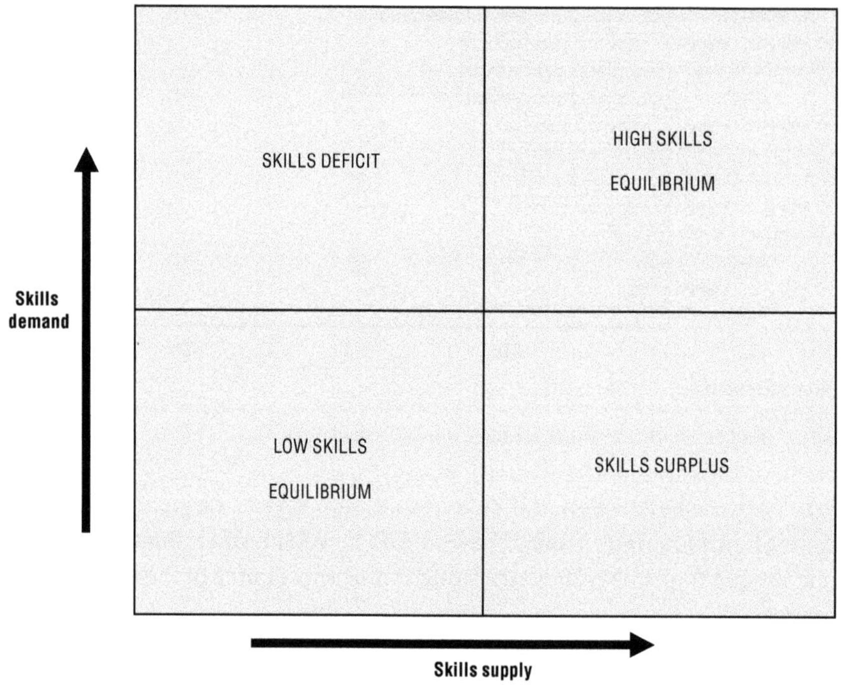

Source: Froy, F. and S. Giguère (2010), "Putting in Place Jobs that Last: A Guide to Rebuilding Quality Employment at Local Level", *OECD Local Economic and Employment Development (LEED) Working Papers*, No. 2010/13, OECD Publishing, *http://dx.doi.org/10.1787/5km7jf7qtk9p-en.*

Looking at the figure above, in the top-left corner (skills gaps and shortages), demand for high skills is met by a supply of low skills, a situation that results in reported skills gaps and shortages. In the top-right corner, demand for high skills is met by an equal supply of high skills resulting in a high-skill equilibrium. This is the most desired destination of all high performing local economies. At the bottom-left corner the demand for low skills is met by a supply of low skills resulting in a low-skill equilibrium. The challenge facing policymakers is to get the economy moving in a north-easterly direction towards the top-right corner. Lastly, in the bottom-right corner, demand for low skills is met by a supply of high skills resulting in an economy where what high skills are available are not utilised. This leads to the out migration of talent, underemployment, skill under-utilisation, and attrition of human capital, all of which signal missed opportunities for creating prosperity.

This typology is applied to economic regions in Saskatchewan using the provincial median for comparison purposes in Figure 5.11. In analysing the results, one can see the Regina – Moose Mountain and falls Saskatoon-Biggar economic regions fall into the high-skills equilibrium quadrant, whereas Swift Current – Moose Jaw and Yorkton-Melville fall into a low-skills equilibrium, which indicates a prevalence of lower quality jobs. One would expect areas around Saskatoon and Regina to fall into a high-skills equilibrium as there is a larger proportion of the population with a high level of skills in these communities. There are

Box 5.1. **Explaining the OECD diagnostic tool comparing skills supply and demand**

The analysis is carried out at Territorial Level 3 regions (regions with populations ranging between 150 000-800 000). The supply of skills was measured by the percentage of the population in employment with postsecondary education. The demand for skills was approximated using a composite index: percentage of the population in employment having medium to high skilled occupations and GVA per worker (weighted at 0.25 and 0.75 respectively). The indices are standardised using the inter-decile method and are compared with the national median. Further explanations on the methodology can be found in Froy, Giguère and Meghnagi, 2012.

Source: Froy, F., S. Giguère and M. Meghnagi (2012), "Skills for Competitiveness: A Synthesis Report", *OECD Local Economic and Employment Development (LEED) Working Papers*, No. 2012/09, OECD Publishing, *http://dx.doi.org/10.1787/5k98xwskmvr6-en.*

challenges associated with this analysis as the regions cover do not necessarily correspond to travel to work areas. It was not possible to collect further disaggregated information due to data comparability issues.

Due to data availability and suppression issues, it was not possible to perform this data analysis in the Yukon.

Figure 5.11. **Balancing the supply and demand of skills, Saskatchewan, 2011**

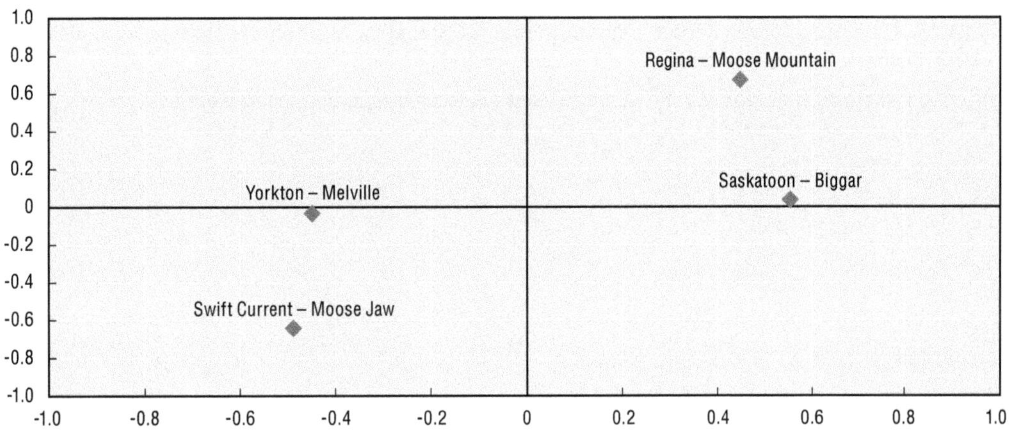

References

Anderson, A. (2004), "Migration and Mobility Between Reserve and City: A Survey of Whitecap Dakota/Sioux First Nations Residents in Saskatoon", University of Saskatchewan, Saskatoon.

City of Saskatoon (2015), "First Nation Community Profile: Whitecap Dakota First Nation", *www.saskatoon.ca/sites/default/files/documents/community-services/planning-development/future-growth/urban-reserves-treaty-land-entitlement/fnp_whitecap_final.pdf.*

City of Whitehorse (2015), "Whitehorse Community Profile", *http://profile.id.com.au/whitehorse.*

Froy, F. and S. Giguère (2010), "Putting in Place Jobs that Last: A Guide to Rebuilding Quality Employment at Local Level", *OECD Local Economic and Employment Development (LEED) Working Papers*, No. 2010/13, OECD Publishing, Paris, *http://dx.doi.org/10.1787/5km7jf7qtk9p-en.*

Froy, F., S. Giguère and M. Meghnagi (2012), "Skills for Competitiveness: A Synthesis Report",*OECD Local Economic and Employment Development (LEED) Working Papers*, No. 2012/09, OECD Publishing, Paris, *http://dx.doi.org/10.1787/5k98xwskmvr6-en*.

Government of Yukon (2015a), "Graduation Rates 2014", *www.education.gov.yk.ca/graduation-rates.html*.

Government of Yukon (2015b), "Yukon economic Outlook: January 2015", Whitehorse, *http://economics.gov.yk.ca/Files/2015/YukonEconomicOutlook_January2015.pdf*.

Hemson Consulting Ltd. (2013), "City of Regina Population, Housing and Employment Forecasts and Land needs analysis to 2041, Final technical memorandum", Toronto.

Klondike Development Organization (2013), "Dawson Employer Labour Market survey Report", Dawson City.

National Resources Canada (2015), *Regina Economic Profile*, Government of Canada, Ottawa.

Regina Regional Opportunities Commission (2015), "Regina Regional Economic Profile", *www.economicdevelopmentregina.com/assets/EconomicProfileAugust2015.pdf*.

Saskatchewan Bureau of Statistics (2015a), *Monthly Statistical Review*, Volume 41, No. 11, November 2015, ISSN 0706–7836, Government of Saskatchewan.

Saskatchewan Bureau of Statistics (2015b), "Economic Review 2014", Number Sixty-Eight, Government of Saskatchewan, *www.stats.gov.sk.ca/stats/ER2014.pdf*.

Skookum Jim Friendship Centre (2015), "About Us", *http://skookumjim.com/about-us/*.

The Canadian Business Journal (2011), "Whitecap Development Corporation", Volume 4, Issue 11, Mississauga.

YSB (2015a), "Population Report", June 2015, Yukon Bureau of Statistics, Whitehorse, *www.eco.gov.yk.ca/fr/pdf/populationJun_2015.pdf*.

YSB (2015b), "Yukon Employment Historical Data 2005-2014", Yukon Bureau of Statistics, Whitehorse, *www.eco.gov.yk.ca/fr/pdf/Historical_LFS_2014_r.pdf*.

YSB (2013), "Business Survey Report", Yukon Bureau of Statistics, Whitehorse, *www.eco.gov.yk.ca/pdf/2013_Business_Survey_Report.pdf*.

Whitecap Dakota First Nation (2015), "About", *www.whitecapdakota.com/about/about-us/*.

Employment and Skills Strategies in Saskatchewan
and the Yukon, Canada

Chapter 6

Key findings from the OECD Local Job Creation Dashboard

This chapter highlights findings from the local job creation dashboard in Saskatchewan and the Yukon. The findings are discussed through the four thematic areas of the study: 1) better aligning policies and programmes to local employment development; 2) adding value through skills; 3) targeting policy to local employment sectors and investing in quality jobs; and 4) being inclusive.

Overview

Each of the four thematic areas of the study is presented and discussed sequentially, accompanied by an explanation of the results. The full results of the OECD Local Job Creation dashboard in Saskatchewan and Yukon are presented in Figure 6.1 and 6.2 below.

Figure 6.1. **Local Job Creation Dashboard for Saskatchewan**

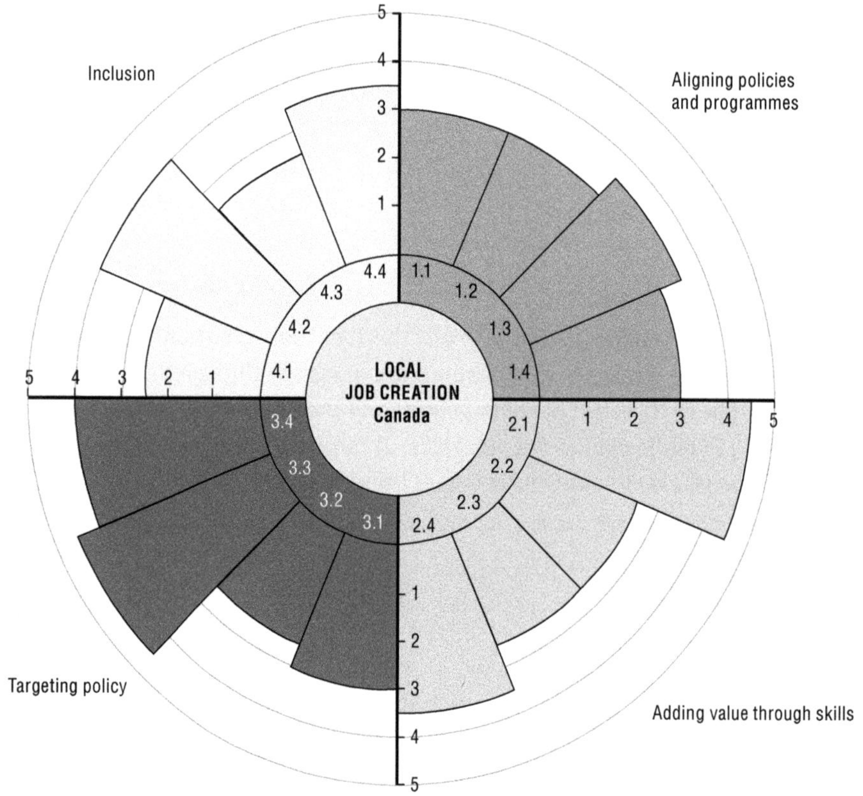

Figure 6.2. **Local Job Creation Dashboard for Yukon**

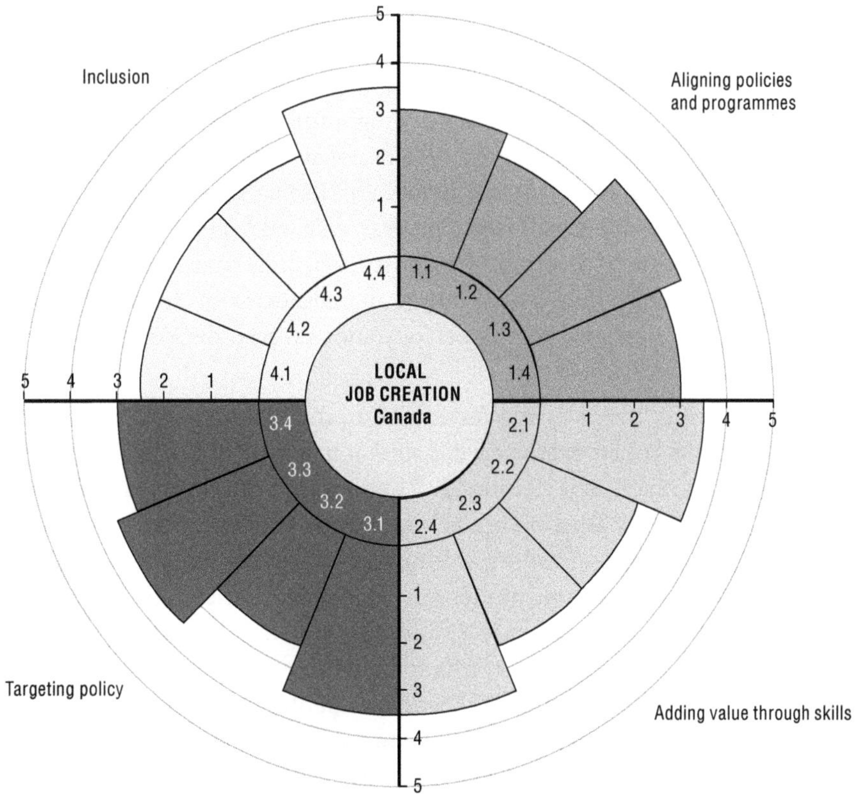

Theme 1: Better aligning policies and programmes to local economic development

Figure 6.3. **Dashboard results for better aligning policies and programmes to local economic development**

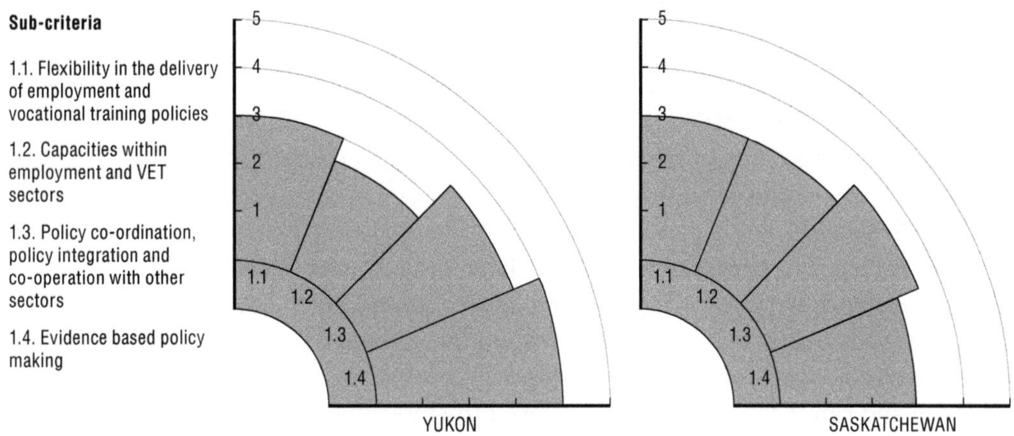

Flexibility within employment services

The OECD defines flexibility as "the possibility to adjust policy at its various design, implementation and delivery stages to make it better adapted to local contexts, actions carried out by other organisations, strategies being pursued, and challenges and opportunities faced" (Giguère and Froy, 2009). Flexibility here refers to the latitude that exists in the management of the employment and training system, rather than the flexibility in the labour market itself.

It is important to differentiate between operational and strategic flexibility. Operational flexibility applies to the delivery of programmes, and refers to the leeway given to individual case officers to decide on the type of policy intervention that should be used to serve an unemployed client. Strategic flexibility applies when the local employment service takes a leadership role in adjusting programmes and policies to their local labour market. The achievement of strategic flexibility requires that national governments provide sufficient latitude when allocating responsibilities in designing policies and programmes; managing budgets; setting performance targets, deciding on eligibility, and outsourcing services (OECD, 2014).

Looking at flexibility between the federal and provincial/territorial level in Canada, both Saskatchewan and Yukon exercise a considerable degree of flexibility in determining how services are organised and delivered. They are provided funds from the federal government to design and administer active labour market programmes. However, flexibility in the use of federal funding is limited in determining client eligibility. Skills development and training delivered under the Labour Market Development Agreements (LMDA) is limited to active and former EI claimants. LMDA funding also supports the provision of employment assistant services for unemployed Canadians, regardless of EI eligibility. Further federal funding for non-EI eligible clients is provided through the Canada Job Fund (CJF) Agreements. The CJF Agreements support a broad range of employment programs and services designed and delivered by provinces and territories, including support to: unemployed persons who are not eligible for Employment Insurance benefits; and employed persons who do not have a high school diploma or recognised certification or who have low levels of literacy and essential skills. These bilateral agreements, as well as the Targeted Initiative for Older Workers, and the Labour Market Agreement for Persons with Disabilities each allow for the province or territory to establish priorities and service arrangements within broad criteria that are designed to avoid making payments for services covered by other arrangements.

As both Saskatchewan and Yukon have significant indigenous populations, additional specialised services are provided through ESDC's Aboriginal Labour Market Programmes. For First Nation communities that have achieved self-government, there are services provided to local residents by the applicable First Nation's administration.

Saskatchewan

In Saskatchewan, basic services are available to all job seekers including access to job boards, assistance with preparing CVs and some counselling by Labour Market Services. For those job seekers who qualify for Employment Insurance or Jobs First as part of Saskatchewan's Transition Benefits (T-Program) Income Assistance, counselling is more extensive and can include testing and referral to employment and training programmes offered by not for profit or educational providers under contract to Labour Market Services. In Regina, there is one central Labour Market services location in the downtown area.

A team of client service consultants in the Labour Market Services office develop contracts with organisations that provide employment, and specific skills development opportunities. Individual referrals for training are made by case managers. In addition to

Labour Market Services operations, job seekers of indigenous background and from rural areas may choose to use facilities at the Newo Yotina Friendship Centre that are funded under the Urban Aboriginal Strategy by INAC to assist them in adapting to city life. Some of the programmes and services of the Centre are directed to helping people prepare for employment and find a job.

For indigenous clients, there is also an additional service point through The Gathering Place operated by The Regina Treaty/Status Indian Services Board of Directors, in co-operation with the File Hills Qu'Appelle Tribal Council and Touchwood Agency Tribal Council. Services include directions in career planning, employment and training. Clients can develop and update resumes and covering letters as well as research job opportunities through the Internet and job postings.

Whitecap is an example of how employment services operate in an indigenous community. The Whitecap administration provides basic employment services to all residents and counseling and training services to members of the First Nation. At Whitecap there is an integrated approach between Income Assistance, Employment and Education and Training staff facilitated by a small number of cases. Services can be much more tailored to an individual's requirements. Should an indigenous citizen decide to look for employment in Saskatoon (a community of 200 000, which is 20 kms from Whitecap) they are supported by the Saskatoon Tribal Council under Urban Labour Force Development programmes.

Programmes and services for non-indigenous job seekers are by and large formulated at the provincial level and applied locally. There is little by way of research on the local labour market that would permit adjusting employment services to Regina's specific local labour market conditions. As the community is relatively small, some adjustments are made in the non-government services through direct contact with employers. It should be noted that this could also be related to lack of awareness or knowledge on what is available from other organisations in the community, such as Regina Chamber of Commerce.

Yukon

Services and programs outside of the self-governing First Nations are developed at the Ministry of Advanced Education and administered locally. Local input is gathered through the Labour Force Framework working groups. There is relatively little strategic flexibility devolved to the local level, which may be reasonable when looking at the relatively small numbers of clients involved.

Yukon contracts out basic employment services to not-for-profit organisations. In Whitehorse, there are three service providers offering basic employment services to all job seekers. Employment Central provides services to the majority of job seekers, with the Association Franco-Yukonaise providing similar services in French and Challenge's Work Information Hub providing services to persons with disabilities. Included in these services are basic job search skills, employment counselling and referral to funding programmes offered by the Advanced Education Branch of the Department of Education. Employment Central and Challenge employment services are located in close proximity, which is seen by staff at Employment Central as a positive opportunity for collaboration in service delivery.

The two self-governing First Nations in Whitehorse (Kwalin Dunn and Ta'an Kwäch'än) each provide services to their citizens including a job board for positions within the First Nation administration and associated development corporations. Counsellors can also approve training for job seekers if that is judged to improve employment prospects. First

Nations citizens can also use Employment Central. The Skookum Jim Friendship Centre provides employment services to all youth between 15-30 years and in transition to work. Services offered include job search tools and resources, career development workshops, and case management by onsite employment co-ordinators.

In Dawson City, Klondike Outreach offers basic employment services including a job board and space to prepare a resume. For EI eligible clients, the staff provide case management. Under the recently signed LMA for persons with disabilities, staff may also provide services to this group but would require additional training. Tr'ondëk Hwëch'in (the self-governing First Nation in Dawson City) provides employment services to its citizens. A job board is accessible at the administrative offices and counsellors can authorise training and short-term placements to gain work experience.

Flexibility within vocational education and training

Saskatchewan

Saskatchewan Labour Market Services counsellors can organise training for EI qualified clients and participants in Saskatchewan under the Income Assistance T-Program. The most generous funding is provided under the LMDAs and individuals must qualify under the provisions of Employment Insurance. Vocational training can take three broad forms: work preparation, basic skills development and polytechnic level training. Under the Saskatchewan T-Program (Work First), basic preparation for work can be authorised as well as some entry-level training. Both of these types of training are provided by not-for-profit organisations under contract with Labour Market Services. More extensive training provided by Saskatchewan Polytechnic is generally only available to EI eligible clients.

In terms of the future planning of training, local organisations in Regina rely on their Board and connections with the Chambers of Commerce to identify growth occupations and sectors. The CEO of the Regina Chamber of Commerce has been effective in motivating members to contribute to a number of local initiatives. Saskatchewan has a unique system of vocational education. Since September 2014, Saskatchewan Polytechnic operates 4 campuses in the larger population centres (e.g. Regina, Moose Jaw, Saskatoon, and Prince Albert). Smaller communities are served by the system of community colleges. Because of the provinces small population, programme planning is conducted at the provincial level. This will mean that some students in Regina may need to take programmes in Moose Jaw or Saskatoon. For Moose Jaw, a bus service is provided from the Regina Campus but for Saskatoon students must board in that city. The planning for changes in local conditions can see some flexibility in locating programmes but this process is necessarily slow.

For indigenous groups, vocational education and training can be authorised by employment and education councillors for those living on the First Nation or by offices run by the Tribal Council operating in the urban centres. In Regina, they are operated by the File Hills Tribal Council and in Saskatoon, the Saskatoon Tribal Council. Training can be for work preparation, entry-level skills, pre-apprenticeship, apprenticeship or technical training.

Yukon

Local employment office staff may refer a client that qualifies and will benefit from training to staff at the Ministry of Advanced Education who assess the case and make a decision. Training at several different levels is available through Yukon College including Skills for Employment, pre apprenticeship and apprenticeship, technical training. In

Dawson City, the local campus is limited by its size and offers adult basic education and college preparation courses. It tries to respond to local business needs by offering specialised short courses.

Capacities within employment and VET sectors

Saskatchewan

Labour Market Services appears to be adequately resourced to handle the volumes of clients. Staff are well trained and motivated and engaged in new initiatives such as outcomes based contract management. During this OECD review, some contractors noted that some clients require a longer time frame to acquire basic skills and the pressure to get people into employment may be counterproductive as people are cycling back into programmes when they are placed in employment without proper skills. Whitecap uses intensive case management and has had an exceptional track record on reducing dependency on income assistance.

The vocational education sector in Saskatchewan is well organised and funded. The arrangement of the Polytechnics and colleges and co-operation between different postsecondary institutions is an example of how a small jurisdiction can develop breadth and depth in the system. The system appears to be responsive to a rapidly growing economy and has proved effective in responding to market demand.

Yukon

Resources at Employment Central and Klondike Outreach appear to be adequate for the client volumes. Klondike Outreach was expecting to receive training before handling Labour Market Programmes for Persons with Disabilities clients. Box 6.1 provides a strong example of efforts that are being made to build local governance capacities within indigenous communities in the Yukon.

Box 6.1. **Building local capacity in Yukon's Indigenous Population**

With the signing of First Nations Self Government Agreements, many First Nations communities realised that a wide variety of leadership, governance and public administration skills specific to Yukon First Nations and their context would need to be developed in order to ensure their success. To meet this need, new programmes were created in partnership between Yukon First Nations, Yukon College, the Yukon Government and the federal Department of Indigenous and Northern Affairs.

First Nations Leadership Training (FNLT) is a collection of five integrated courses designed to provide Yukon First Nation leaders, either elected, appointed, or future, with a basic grounding in governance and public administration. The top priority of the programme is to help prepare current and future citizens for their roles as government leaders and community advocates. Each course within the FNLT programmes involves approximately eight hours of instruction. The emphasis in course delivery is on flexibility and responsiveness to the requirements of Yukon First Nations. Yukon College works with individual First Nations to deliver instructional materials in the manner best suited to their needs. The College improves access to this programme by offering both community delivered and Whitehorse-based deliveries to general audiences to develop and improve First Nations governing capacity.

Box 6.1. **Building local capacity in Yukon's Indigenous Population** *(cont.)*

The First Nations Governance and Public Administration (FNGPA) programme (Yukon College, 2011) is a joint initiative between Yukon First Nations, Yukon government and Yukon College and is focused on building capacity and providing senior management staff the tools to enhance the operations of governments in Yukon. It is a made-in-Yukon approach that incorporates local knowledge and experience and recognises the unique Yukon governance landscape.

The programme was developed and expanded from an earlier Executive Development programme which was spearheaded by the Champagne and Aishihik First Nations (CAFN) and focused on CAFN citizens. The certificate programme covers the following course topics: Public Administration; Governance and Land Claims; Community and Economic Development; Human Resource Management; Communications; Management and Strategic Planning; Power and Influence; Accountability and Financial Management; Public Policy; and Intergovernmental Relations

Programme content has been well received across Canada, with the courses being transferable to a number of academic institutions, including Camosun College, Simon Fraser University, and the universities of British Columbia, Victoria, Lethbridge, and Northern BC. Discussions are currently taking place with the University of Saskatchewan about building on this programme to develop an integrated degree programme in Northern Governance and Development.

Course delivery is varied and may include lectures, seminars, presentations, group discussions, hands-on document use, and other participatory activities. Guest speakers and current and past First Nations leaders share personal experiences and contribute additional perspectives.

Policy co-ordination, policy integration and co-operation with other sectors

Saskatchewan

At the provincial level, overall direction is provided through the Saskatchewan Plan for Growth: Vision 2020 and Beyond. In Saskatchewan, the Premier is focused on this plan, which emphasises building "on the strength of Saskatchewan's people, resources and innovation" and has ensured its communication throughout the Province. During this OECD review, interlocutors from the government, private sector and non-government organisations all referenced the plan. The Plan has resonance for two reasons. First, Saskatchewan is a comeback story; having been a province of declining population and prospects, it has become an engine in recent years with above average growth and below average unemployment. The second is strong leadership, as during the course of this OECD review, several interviewees cited leadership as a significant factor in the province's current position as a top performing jurisdiction.

The Saskatchewan Plan for Growth has specific actions that guide Ministries in formulating their individual plans and signal areas of horizontal activity. Labour market services, some vocational training functions, and economic development are located within the Ministry of the Economy. The integration of these activities at the provincial level provides the opportunity for the integration of policies and programmes locally. The Ministry of the Economy 2014-15 Annual Plan describes the following strategies:

1. Increase investment and international engagement in Saskatchewan
2. Create a sustainable competitive business environment
3. Increase entrepreneurship in Saskatchewan
4. Increase resource production and manage industry activity
5. Manage resources to ensure conservation, fairness, public safety and environmental sustainability
6. Develop the knowledge and skills of Saskatchewan's people
7. Attract skilled and knowledgeable workers from across Canada and the world
8. Retain knowledgeable and skilled workers in Saskatchewan workplaces and communities

Looking more specifically at Regina, there are no formal mechanisms for bringing together local employment and training actors. The Regina city administration does not play an active role in the city's labour market activities; and the Saskatchewan Government does not have local community based mechanisms such as work force planning boards or community based tables to coordinate local activity. Labour Market Services has significant contact with individual operations through contract issuing and monitoring but does not play a convening role at the local level.

Looking at the co-ordination between Service Canada offices, which administer unemployment benefits through EI Part I funding and the active labour market programmes, recent changes have resulted in the processing of claims in multiple locations and in some cases local Regina staff report to supervisors in locations outside the Province. Contact between Service Canada and Labour Market Services is sporadic. In cases where individuals wish claims to be reviewed and seek the assistance of an advocate, it can be difficult to connect with the right people in Service Canada.

There are a number of policies and programmes affecting Saskatchewan's indigenous population that are handled at the Federal, provincial and local levels. There does not appear to be a mechanism to bring the various actors together to discuss common objectives and co-ordinate activities in Regina around indigenous activities.

In Whitecap, the single administration makes the integration of various participants in the community easier (see Box 6.2). The First Nations Community has a land use and economic development plan that drives its labour force development activities. For those who leave the community to go to Saskatoon or Regina, they may choose to use services provided through Labour Market Services, those of a nongovernmental organisation such as a friendship centre or a dedicated service provided by the Tribal Council.

Box 6.2. **Policy Co-ordination in Whitecap First Nations**

One of the most significant differences between Canada's indigenous population and the general population is the rate at which students successfully complete high school. Twenty years ago, the Whitecap Dakota First Nation high school completion rates were not at the provincial standard. The recently elected chief at that time saw education as one of the important reforms that would make a difference in his community. Whitecap operated the school on-reserve with funding provided by Indigenous and Northern Affairs Canada. After grade six, students would be bussed to a high school 20 kilometers away in Saskatoon. Many Whitecap First Nation students did not perform well at high school as they were not prepared and lacked the essential literacy and math skills to master new material. As a first

Box 6.2. **Policy Co-ordination in Whitecap First Nations** *(cont.)*

phase of reform, primary school children were given extra tutoring to help ready them for the transition. Both high schools and elementary schools transitioning the WDFN students were making an effort to become more welcoming places of learning. Teachers at both schools, tutors and parents worked to make educating Whitecaps' children a priority.

This level of collaboration has produced a significant increase in the student success rate. Looking for additional improvements Whitecap approached the Saskatoon Board to have its primary school included as part of the Saskatoon Board. This was a complicated process that involved the federal government filling a funding gap of CAD 3 000 per student per year – the difference between what the Saskatoon Board spends and the funding allocation for the Reserve school. Importantly, the Saskatoon Board had to ensure that curriculum provided education in the culture of the Whitecap Dakota First Nation.

Benefits of the partnership include:

- Students are part of a fully integrated primary and high school system with the resources of the Saskatoon Board; and
- Teachers at Whitecap as employees of the Saskatoon School Public Schools are part of the Saskatchewan Teachers Federation with the professional development and career mobility benefits of that system.

A further noteworthy benefit of the partnership is the enhancement of early learning for the youngest citizens of the WDFN. An Early Learning Center is under construction that will provide a learning and care centre for 56 of the youngest WDFN members, The entire elementary school has been brought to provincial standards as a facility.

The student success rate for Whitecap citizens is now approaching those of the general school population with many graduates continuing on to postsecondary studies. An increasing number of Whitecap First Nations university graduates are taking on management positions in the community as well as in larger companies and in the broader Canadian labour market.

Yukon

Yukon's labour market activities are based on a Labour Market Framework, which was initiated in 2008 and combines a far-reaching series of stakeholder committees covering four thematic areas of the territory's labour market strategy, including comprehensive skills and training; immigration; labour market information; and recruitment and employee retention

Stakeholders play an active role in informing the on-going policy discussion around labour market issues and programme design and implementation. One of the key features of the framework is to look for greater vertical (between different orders of governments) and horizontal integration (among different Ministries in Yukon). A good example is recent efforts to increase the employability and job prospects for those on income assistance. The Ministry of Social Services has recently added a caseworker to strengthen efforts in employment and training assistance. There are about 800 non-indigenous persons on social assistance in Yukon. Currently, it is not clear how many of these individuals are able to find work. The caseworker's role is to strengthen connections with the college to increase training, labour market services like Employment Central and employers to find job opportunities. The programme is generous both in terms of its training and subsidy level (e.g. wage subsidies can last for up to one year).

The framework approach is a promising practice that could be looked at by a number of Canadian jurisdictions as well as international partners in this OECD study. There are challenges in developing the approach. Originally, the Framework consisted of five focus areas but has more recently been reduced to four. The smaller number makes for a more manageable series of working groups. Getting the right balance of participants both in terms of breadth of actors but as well as level of actors is important. During this OECD review, some interviewees from both governmental and non-governmental organisations were accompanied by supervisors or deferred to supervisors suggesting that some working group members may be quite junior. One person interviewed suggested that discussions did not usually lead to a decision and this affected on-going interest in the process.

The Framework covers all of the Yukon, which is rational given the small size of the jurisdiction but there are increased capabilities at the local level in the two communities studied. As some of the challenges of these communities are uniquely local such as high levels of seasonal employment in Dawson City, there may be some scope to build a local dimension into the framework.

Each First Nation in the Yukon has its own employment and training division as part of its administration. Services are loosely connected to those offered through the Yukon government and citizens can choose to use general services or those specifically connected to the First Nation administration. Services tend to be highly integrated and may involve tight co-operation between the First Nation development corporation and the employment and training division. The administration can even act as the record keeper for apprenticeships. Education while provided through the College responds to the requirements of the First Nation administration that works closely with the College to ensure sufficient enrolments and support for students.

Evidence-based policy making

Saskatchewan

Information is mostly available at a provincial level of aggregation. The Saskatchewan Bureau of Statistics is the authoritative source of data used by government agencies. The Bureau collaborates with Statistics Canada and uses the Census and Labour Force Survey for its principal statistics on employment. Industry data uses both Statistics Canada surveys as well as those from Industry Canada.

The City of Regina provides some demographic information on its web site; however the most extensive report is from 2008. *Focusing on People* is a report developed jointly by the City, the United Way, Police Services, the Health Region and the Regional Inter-sectoral Committee. The focus on provincial statistics reflects planning for Labour Market Services, Advanced Education, Economy and Social Services and the fact that these services are delivered by the province rather than by the City. The Economic Development area has a stronger local focus with the Regina Regional Opportunities Commission that has an economic development plan for Regina, which is based on the City of Regina population, housing and employment forecasts, as well as an analysis of those industrial sectors that offer the best opportunities for the city.

Yukon

Information is available at both the Yukon-wide level and community level through the Yukon Bureau of Statistics. Data is used to inform government initiatives on a territory wide basis. Because of its small size, Yukon collects data to supplement Statistics Canada's regular surveys.

In both Whitehorse and Dawson, local plans have been produced using data relevant to those communities. These local plans address concerns such as employment, skills development and economic activity. In Whitehorse, the plan was developed by the city, led by the economic development department, in Dawson the city plan has been put together by the Klondike Development Organisation which is a partnership between the city of Dawson, the Dawson City Chamber of Commerce, Klondike Visitors Association, the City Arts Society and Chief Isaac Inc.

The Yukon Government has a well-developed evaluation culture and uses the results of its evaluations to modify programmes and activities. Specific changes to the employment development activities in the income assistance programme were as a result of a recent evaluation. The orientation of Northern Research Institute is being fine-tuned based on findings from a 2013 evaluation. Other relevant evaluations to this study include School of Visual Arts 2015, Labour Market Agreements Evaluations 2013, and Yukon Nominee Programme Evaluation 2011.

Local capacity to acquire data is limited and the ability to draw down and use data from the Yukon Bureau of Statistics is also somewhat limited. However, given the small size of the jurisdiction. Whitehorse and indeed Dawson City can base their activities on local relevant information.

Theme 2: Adding value through skills

Figure 6.4. **Dashboard results for adding value through skills**

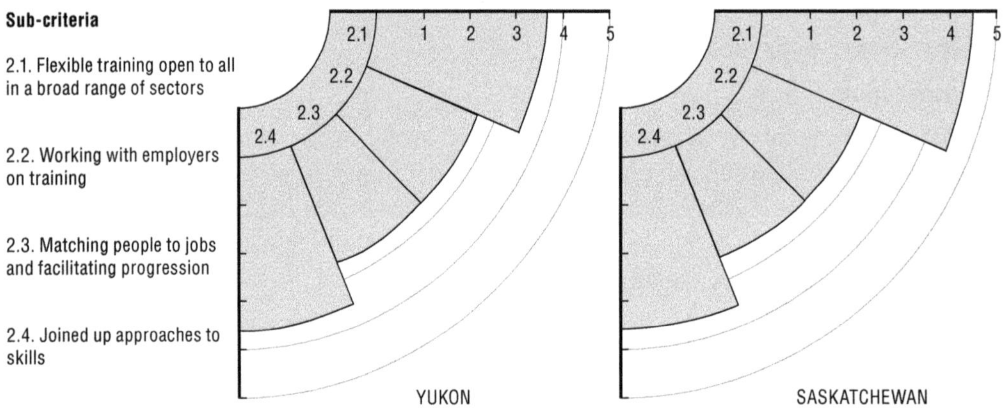

Flexible training open to all in a broad range of sectors

Saskatchewan

Saskatchewan has a unique postsecondary system that is organised around skills disciplines, geography and has a specialised capacity for indigenous students. In the four major urban centres, there are Polytechnics. Polytechnics offer predominately certificates, diplomas and degrees in professional and technical disciplines. For courses offered in Moose Jaw there is a shuttle service. Saskatoon is two hours from Regina and it is possible that students would be required to board in Saskatoon for some programmes. In communities without a polytechnic organisation, there are community colleges. However, no community in Saskatchewan can have both a college and a polytechnic.

In addition to the polytechnic schools, Regina has an entry level trades facility at Regina Trades and Skills. At this school, students must go through a competitive process to gain entry and follow a programme developed in close collaboration with Regina businesses and are assured a job on graduation. Tuition is free and students are paid while they learn. A normal year sees 2 cohorts of students: one from January-June designed to release qualified graduates for the construction season; and, one from August-January. Each course takes a maximum of 14 students and focuses on instructor-led hands-on training. Regina has two universities: the University of Regina and the First Nations University of Canada.

The Saskatchewan Apprenticeship and Trades Certification Commission manages apprenticeships. *The Apprenticeship and Trade Certification Act* 1999 authorises the Commission to manage the Apprenticeship and Trade Certification system. *The Act* gives the Commission the authority to make regulations to ensure the efficient and effective operation of the apprenticeship system to meet the needs of industry in a timely manner. A small percentage of the Polytechnic students (about 15%) are in apprenticeship programmes. Most students in the Regina Skills and Trades programme can move into apprenticeships.

Indigenous people have additional pathways through the Saskatchewan Indian Institute of Technology (see Box 6.3). SIIT Regina has approximately 200 students and a total of twenty-four staff between two campus locations, Regina Campus and Construction Careers Campus. Many of the students are from diverse backgrounds that include Metis, Lakota, Dakota, Nakoda, Saulteaux and Cree.

Box 6.3. **Saskatchewan Indian Institute of Technology**

Established in 1976, the Saskatchewan Indian Institute of Technologies (SIIT) is one of the four Saskatchewan educational institutions with credit granting authority. The Institute is governed by First Nations leaders and representatives from across the province.

SIIT offers certificate and diploma programmes in the trades and industrial areas, business and technology, health and community studies, and adult basic education to over 2 400 students annually. Programming is delivered through three principal campuses in Regina, Saskatoon and Prince Albert, plus eight Career Centres and a number of learning centres located throughout the province. SIIT also operates the Saskatchewan Aviation Learning Centre at the Saskatoon airport.

SIIT strives to be the institute of choice for First Nations learners. Approximately 93% of current students are indigenous, First Nations, Metis or Non-Status Indian. SIIT is also committed to building and maintaining strong relationships and partnerships with a growing range of provincial and national industry leaders, professional associations and academic institutions.

In Whitecap, the vision has been to build a strong attachment to education (see previous Box 6.2). This facilitates the transition to high school in Saskatoon where all students continue their education. Additional support is offered to students to ensure high graduation rates. Whitecap residents have access to facilities that are organised in a similar fashion to those in Regina. Saskatoon is Saskatchewan's largest city and has a greater postsecondary population so each of the institutions has a larger student population. SIIT main campus is in Saskatoon.

Yukon

Yukon has one college that handles the complete range of students from adult basic education through technical and trades training and even some courses that can be articulated into a bachelor's degree. In order to meet such a broad mandate, the college has had to make important decisions about where to invest in programing and where to partner with other institutions. The college is part of both British Columbia's and Alberta's credit transfer programmes allowing students to transfer from the college to any college or university in those two provinces. Yukon College is unique in having an agreement with two provinces. Most students moving on from Yukon College will study in the provinces of British Columbia or Alberta.

The college offers a wide variety of technical and trades training that is focused on growth areas in Yukon's economy. For those that are looking for a pathway back into higher education there are adult education and pre-apprenticeship courses. The college has a large and innovative First Nations programme mandate that is focused on supporting self-government among Yukon's fourteen First Nations (see previous Box 6.1). The First Nations leadership training is unique in its focus and is widely seen as an important part of building long-term success at the community level and ensuring the depth of leadership needed to govern all aspects of devolved responsibilities. All staff and students irrespective of their role at the college must take a one-day class on Yukon's First Nation's history and culture. This is seen as important in promoting broad cohesion in Yukon's work force and among its citizens.

There is a small campus of the College at Dawson, Tr'odëk Hätr'unohtän Zho (Klondike Learning House). Learners can upgrade their adult basic education skills and take college preparation level courses, offered on campus or by videoconference, enabling students to pursue their career goals. A variety of short and long-term training programmes are offered with a priority given to trades training to meet local employment needs. Finally through the Dawson City Campus' affiliation with the Klondike Institute of Art and Culture (KIAC) and the Yukon School of Visual Arts (YSOVA), its sister campus, dozens of artistic, creative and special interest options are available to community members. There are still a significant number of students who chose to study at the main campus in Whitehorse or outside Yukon.

Working with employers on training

With skills shortages being increasingly reported in a number of Canada's industries, there is more emphasis being placed on employers and their role in the overall performance of the labour market. Demographic effects are suggesting Canadian workers will need to be increasingly productive in order to ensure a continued high standard of living. Shortages are a regular and important feature of the rapidly growing economies of both Saskatchewan and Yukon.

Saskatchewan

Labour Market Services in Regina work primarily with job seekers. During interviews conducted for this OECD review, staff indicated a desire to do more work with employers but as of yet employer contact is limited. Non-governmental organisations under contract with Labour Market Services do engage local employers as part of their placement services following employment preparation and development activities. Local stakeholders indicated that they most often work with employers where they have well developed relationships.

Saskatchewan Polytechnic's hallmark is its focus on labour market demand. For new programmes, a requirement is an assessment of labour market need supported by employer demand. For existing programmes, there is an annual review of all activities. The Polytechnic uses 800 industry experts to make recommendations on the optimal sizing of programmes and on curriculum. The metrics that Saskatchewan Polytechnic focuses on are graduate employment (currently 95% employed six months after graduation) and employer satisfaction. In addition 92% of graduates stay within the province indicating that the mechanisms employed by the Polytechnic to anticipate employer requirements are working. Saskatchewan Polytechnic works at a province wide level rather than being focused on particular local labour markets.

Saskatchewan Indian Institute of Technology has processes similar to Sask Polytech and in fact partners with the Polytechnic on delivery of a number of courses. The critical difference for SIIT is that in addition to employer requirements, it focuses on the unique requirements of its indigenous student population.

Regina Trades and Skills Centre is focused on the Regina labour market and is quite responsive to employer needs (see Box 6.4). Working closely with the Regina Chamber of Commerce, it has a board of local business owners. Trades and Skills looks to place all graduates and uses the specific requirements of hiring companies as a way of adding specific employer value around courses that qualify for apprenticeship under the Saskatchewan Apprenticeship and Certification Commission.

Box 6.4. **Regina Trades and Skills Centre**

Regina Trades and Skills Centre (RTSC) opened in 2007 when the Saskatchewan government provided funding, which had been announced as part of the Revitalizing Neighbourhoods initiative in 2006, for industry led, short-term trades and skills programmes aimed at employment and/or further postsecondary training. The Regina Trades and Skills Centre was established as a not-for-profit Corporation overseen by a community board composed of 14 business and public sector leaders. RTSC has two main goals:

- Deliver short-term trades and skills training that lead to entry-level jobs in industries where workers are in high demand; and
- Work with industry to develop and deliver relevant and recognised programmes that are responsive to industry needs for trained and skilled workers.

Regina Trades and Skills Centre courses are taught by experienced tradespeople. Course offerings change throughout the year and stay attuned to the demands of the current labour market. Courses run from 8-10 weeks in length and follow an "earn while you learn" model. Current offerings range across such fields as culinary arts, flooring installation, commercial concrete, electrical, carpentry, bricklaying and scaffolding. All RTSC courses include specific occupational training, both practical and theoretical and training in Occupational Health and Safety and Workplace Essential Skills. Programme Co-ordinators work with employers to link course participants to jobs prior to the completion of training.

Many of the courses at the Centre lead to jobs that are in high demand in the province. For example, participants often go on to apprenticeships with their employers. There are about 100 individuals who go through the programme each session. Completion rates for students top 90% with many programmes experiencing 100% completion rates. Average employment rates top 90% as well, with many experiencing 100% employment upon graduation.

Whitecap is focused on employer requirements. It is itself a large employer (300 employees on the First Nation) and as such can signal requirements directly through its education and training division. Its economic development corporation looks for partnerships that can produce employment opportunities for its citizens.

Yukon

The contracted employment services have only limited contact with employers. During interviews conducted for this OECD review, Employment Central expressed that this is something it would like to expand. Social Services expressed the same desire and Challenge contacts employers in the context of its employment development efforts with the view of placing clients.

Yukon College is developing its employer network as part of strengthening its internal culture of planning and performance management. The College must respond to a broad series of priorities that include high public sector job demand for professional, technical and administrative personnel and an emergent need for leadership development among self-governing First Nations communities. The other pull for the college is its status as Yukon's College and needing to focus broadly on those areas of the territorys' economy where there is strong demand. This creates tensions between local Whitehorse employer priorities and broader territorial priorities. A demand driven initiative that is associated with the College and funded under ESDC's ASET programme is the Yukon Mine Training Association (YMTA). YMTA is a collaboration between Yukon First Nations and the mining industry to increase the number of indigenous peoples who work in Yukon mines.

In Dawson City, the College has limited flexibility as it primary mission is to prepare students for higher education programmes and deliver programmes with strong local needs, driven primarily by the mining and tourism sectors. Tr'ondëk Hwëch'in works closely with the Dawson City campus to create training opportunities for its citizens (The City of Dawson and Tr'ondëk Hwëch'in, 2007). One innovation is that the First Nation contracts apprentices from its community and can keep the record of hours towards the apprenticeship irrespective of what job site or supervising journeyperson working with the apprentice (see Box 6.5). There are no private providers of training in Yukon. One company that had investigated the possibility of opening a school in Whitehorse indicated that the small population and high levels of subsidisation for publicly offered programmes would make it diffcult for a private operator to function.

Box 6.5. **Tr'ondëk Hwëch'in apprenticeship registration**

Finding skilled trades in Dawson City can be challenging because of its remote location. In spite of the demand, it is hard to encourage trades people to settle in the community. As most businesses in Dawson City are small, it is equally difficult for an apprentice to complete a programme with a single employer. A number of residents in Dawson City have begun but not completed their apprenticeship training.

To help increase the number of apprenticeship completions and to make it easier for both apprentices and employers, the Tr'ondëk Hwëch'in administration registers apprentices and keeps the apprentices log. The programme is starting small and has around 10 individuals registered. It is hoped that by minimising the administrative burden for employers and recognizing that apprentices will move between employers to get their necessary training the overall number of completions in the community will increase.

Matching people to jobs and facilitating progression

In both Saskatchewan and Yukon, employed and unemployed individuals have access to the Job Bank (*www.jobbank.gc.ca*), which is administered by Service Canada. This web portal provides an electronic listing of jobs provided by employers from everywhere across Canada. It includes training, career, and worker information to help provide individuals with information on potential career opportunities as well as the required skills and knowledge to work in various occupations and sectors. In some interviews, it was felt that the national service represented a poor reflection of the local job situation and that many employers would not post positions on the national system. For jobs where temporary foreign workers may be sought, there is a requirement to post and it was stated that locals would ignore these postings knowing that they would not get serious consideration.

Saskatchewan

Saskatchewan is shifting to outcomes based contracting that will focus on people being retained in employment six months after placement. This will focus attention on effective placements for those NGOs who are under contract to Labour Market Services. The fact that Saskatchewan has been a tight labour market for a number of years does create some distortions that may result in longer-term problems. Because wages can be relatively high for semi-skilled workers in the extraction industries, workers who have reached an age where their bodies cannot take the stress of this labour face difficult transitions. Youth may forgo education in favour of an immediate good paying job that can result in limited career mobility. For public employment services, more of their clients face multiple barriers and placements can be more challenging or employment preparation may take longer. During this OECD review, interviewees pointed to all of these challenges and suggested that some additional flexibility could be helpful in better serving clients.

Career guidance is well established in Saskatchewan's secondary schools as part of a provincial effort to retain young people in the province. Postsecondary institutions, government departments and industry ensure young people have good information to make labour market decisions and to ensure that postsecondary educational pathways are clearly articulated into either college or university. Efforts are made along with high school career counselling often in the second year of secondary education to create awareness of college offerings. A number of dual credit programmes are being offered that allow high school students to complete their studies while at the same time begin a Polytechnic programme. Dual credit allows you to earn a Saskatchewan high school credit and Saskatchewan Polytechnic credit at the same time.

Generalised labour market information plays a less important role in high demand sectors that engage in active recruiting. Companies use recruiters and social media as tools in their search for qualified talent. The Skills and Trades Centres are examples of where employers are becoming more active in training and in return get the opportunity to offer promising students work placements on graduation. During this OECD review, interviewees indicated that tightening the link between employers training is an effective way to ensure job readiness on graduation.

Yukon

The Yukon labour market is characterised by high demand for skilled employees in particular in public and First Nations administrations, demand in some skilled trades and selective requirements for entry-level personnel in the retail and service sectors. The other feature of the labour market is a high rate of seasonality. This is particularly apparent in Dawson City.

For skilled workers, there are significant incentives for employers to recruit individuals with a good fit for jobs. The tightness of the labour market promotes internal mobility within organisations. For unskilled workers the situation is less attractive. Without EI qualification, they have little access to training and are more likely to resort to seasonal work.

Yukon has invested in a local labour market information system called YUWIN. During this OECD review, it was indicated that employers seem to like the system for its simplicity and ease of use as do employment services personnel who see it as an effective product. The Yukon government is considering dropping YUWIN in favour of the national job bank. Concern was expressed during the interviews that the national system will not work as effectively.

There are three programme streams under the Canada-Yukon Job Fund Agreement; the Canada-Yukon Job Grant, Employment Services and Supports, and Employer-Sponsored Training.

1. *Canada-Yukon Job Grant (CYJG)*: This programme supports employers interested in investing in training for current or future employees. Training may be offered by colleges, trade union centres or private trainers. Training can take place in a classroom, a workplace or online. Costs are shared by the employer and Advanced Education.
2. *Employment Services and Supports (ESS)*: This programme continues the services that were offered under the Labour Market Agreement. This program helps unemployed or low-skilled individuals who need support to enter the labour market. Eligible programmes may include, but are not limited to skills training, such as training in literacy and numeracy or advanced skills training, on-the-job training, job readiness assistance, financial supports and benefits such as loans, grants and living allowances, employment counselling and services, labour market connections and services that promote and enhance labour market efficiency.
3. *Employer-Sponsored Training (EST)*: This programme has a broader scope for training activities and costs. It provides more diverse opportunities than the Canada-Yukon Job Grant. Yukon is first implementing the Canada-Yukon Job Grant and Employment Services and Supports. Employer-Sponsored Training will be developed at a later date. The Yukon-Canada Job Grant replaces a preexisting Yukon grant so it is not possible to tell at this early point whether a broader reach of benefits has been achieved in the new agreement.

Joined up approaches to skills

Saskatchewan

Saskatchewan has a strong focus on developing skills across the province. As highlighted earlier in the report, the Saskatchewan Plan for Growth integrates skills development in the broader context of economic development but also in terms of increasing earning power and well-being of the provincial labour force. Bringing together labour market and economic development programmes in the Ministry of Economy is one way in which the province is operationalising this vision. The postsecondary institutions – in particular Saskatchewan Polytechnic and SIIT – organise programming around labour market demand. As mentioned earlier, during this OECD review, interviewees routinely referred to the Plan for Growth as a cornerstone of operational planning.

Despite the success of the Plan for Growth, local co-ordination in Regina is weak. In part, this is the result of having services such income assistance administered by the province, which creates less incentive for the city to convene various employment service providers. During this OECD review, service providers indicated at one time the province was active in convening local agencies but this has not happened in recent years. There exists good capability in the city as demonstrated when the municipality took on the issue of inadequate housing. Efforts are beginning on the local economic development front with RROC looking to build an economic development plan linked to the city's Official Community Plan: Design Regina (City of Regina, 2013).

Design Regina contains a comprehensive policy framework that will guide the physical, environmental, economic, social and cultural development of the city. As such, it plays a key role in setting the long-term direction for Regina and is essential to managing future growth, development and change in the community. The RROC 2015 Business plan is starting the process of identifying key employment growth areas for the city and the skills profile needed to foster that growth. It is still at early stages and this is the time to join up various elements of local employment and inclusion with economic development.

During this OECD review, three specific areas of potential benefit for joined up activity were identified in the local interviews. The first relates to the number of employment service operations that are now serving Regina's indigenous community. Here there may be potential for local operators to identify constructive collaborations. Among organisations that may be interested in looking at synergies are the Friendship Centre, File Hills Qu'Appelle Tribal Council, SIIT Career Centre, Regina Work Prep, and Labour Force Services.

The second relates to changes in the client profile in particular among "multi-barriered" clients. Here two dimensions of work were identified as changing and needing collective attention: Co-ordination of services provided by multiple organisations and varying flexibility between programmes in particular around the total length of time support may need to be provided. A second dimension is around employer engagement and building a network of supportive employers.

The final dimension is aligning locally provided training to key employment growth areas and further strengthening what are already good employer training provider relations. The area identified for development is the link between economic planning and institutional planning. Included in this dimension would be connections between the Saskatchewan Immigrant Nominee Program (SINP) and employment and skills planning.

Yukon

Co-ordination in Yukon occurs through the Labour Market Strategy Framework. The Framework brings together key federal, territorial and municipal agencies in addition to local non-governmental organisations. The working committees for the framework are connected directly to the policy units in the Ministry of Advanced Education and provide a tight feedback loop for consultation during policy formulation/co-ordination and programme design.

The Framework represents a significant effort to join up the many elements of labour market strategy both vertically and horizontally. From all points of examination, it has merit and has helped move Yukon forward both in coordinating policy coming from different levels of government and across Ministries in Yukon. Additionally and perhaps more interestingly from a longer term perspective, it represents a platform that could be used to structure innovative approaches with the participation of stakeholders (policy co-production).

Yukon's economy is driven by public expenditure. In the future, the private sector and nongovernmental sectors will need to develop a greater place in the territory's economy. The framework and its committees could play a role in promoting this shift by increasing the business and non-governmental voice on the committees. Part of what would be needed to do this is to structure meetings that are more familiar to a business culture (e.g. they are tightly focused and proceed to a decision point).

There appears to be some tension between the use of the Yukon Nominee Program (YNP) for entry-level service and retail jobs and efforts to train and connect those residents who are distant from the labour market with employment opportunities. During this OECD review, some interviewees reported that jobs that used to be available to clients are now routinely given to Temporary Foreign Workers. This issue might offer an opportunity to use the platform for innovative collaborations.

There is emerging capacity and strength at the local level that are not fully exploited through the Framework in its current form. Both Whitehorse and Dawson City have developed plans for their local economies. Recognising the mechanisms of local co-ordination explicitly in the Framework would help advance local development. There may be missed opportunities to localise some policy and delivery flexibility locally. One example is the dominance of seasonal employment in Dawson City and a need to look at and plan for both the long-term consequences on individuals as they age in a seasonal work environment as well the short-term impacts of periods of high unemployment. Whitehorse has just produced its Integrated Community Sustainability Plan and there are opportunities for local Whitehorse level co-ordination within the overall Framework (City of Whitehorse, 2015).

Theme 3: Targeting policy to local employment sectors and investing in quality jobs

Figure 6.5. **Dashboard results for targeting policy to local employment sectors and investing in quality jobs**

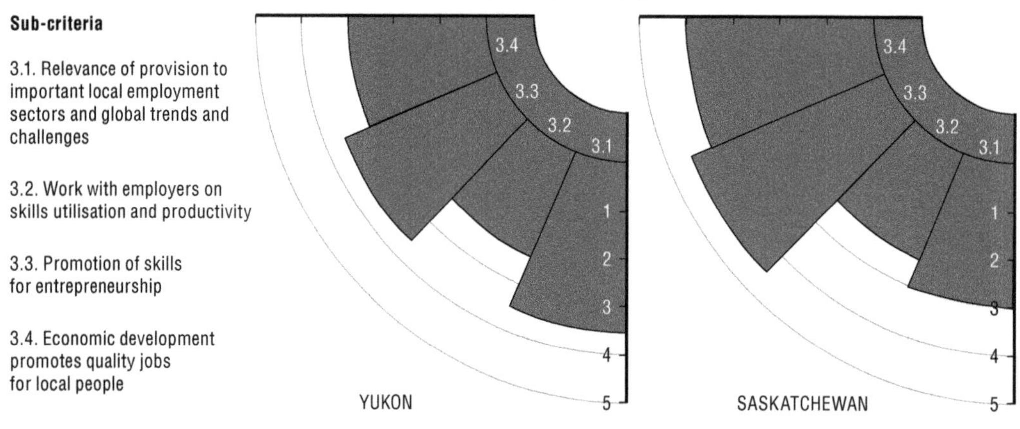

Relevance of provision to important local employment sectors and global trends and challenges

Saskatchewan

Saskatchewan plans at the provincial level and takes a "jurisdictional advantage" approach to its innovation strategy. This approach identifies the core engines of the economy, those areas that drive growth and sustain the province over the long term. It is an evidence-based process that identifies the unique strengths, weaknesses and opportunities that define the province's sustainable advantage. The focus on government investments in innovation is driven from this framework. Three broad sectors are the focus including mining; oil and gas; and, agriculture with selective entry in a few other areas. In each of these areas the province has world-class technologies and companies with global scope.

Innovation Saskatchewan is the government's innovation focal point working closely with the Universities and Saskatchewan Polytechnic. At the local level in Regina, RROC is looking to develop the city's economy by focusing on ecosystem strengths within the city's business community. This top down bottom up approach appears to have merit and can be effective if sufficient flexibilities exist to make necessary accommodations for Regina's unique needs. A concrete example of activity is the construction of the Global Transportation Hub and its attendant requirements for innovation in the logistics sector.

Whitecap is pursuing its strategy along similar lines of looking for jurisdictional advantage which is expressed in two areas: its proximity to Saskatoon; and, its special status with respect to being able to establish partnerships where indigenous content matters. In Whitecap's case, it is in the highly competitive field of resort and entertainment management, having constructed a casino and golf course on its lands.

Yukon

Yukon realises that its efforts in innovation will be small in scale and therefore need to be focused. The Yukon Research Centre looks to make its contributions in the area of cold climate technologies looking to the natural advantage of its location and the multiplier effects that innovations in northern technologies will have on the Yukon economy and Yukon citizens (see Box 6.6).

Box 6.6. **Collaboration among Industry, Accademia and Governments to develop cold climate technology**

Two of Yukon's innate characteristics, climate and remote location – have created a necessity to adapt and to innovate. In the process of overcoming unique challenges, Yukon has leveraged its knowledge sector into world leaders in cold climate technologies. Local Industry, academic research and government support for innovation and entrepreneurship have worked together to produce some outstanding successes. A good example is Icefield Tools in Whitehorse. Borehole drilling is a common technique for determining the size of ore bodies in mineral exploration. Holes are drilled into the ground, pulled out and the core samples examined to see what is inside.

The difficulty is that when you attempt to drill straight down, the hole does not end up being perfectly straight and errors of 45 meters are common even over short drilling distances. This means the ore body may be far from where it was expected to be. Similar challenges exist is positioning drill bits for oil and gas exploration.

It was the early 1990s, when glaciological researcher Erik Blake was drilling through ice in pursuit of his PhD he developed a tool that was so effective at pin pointing the drill bit that it sparked immediate demand. By the early 2000s, he had created technology for the mining industry under the name "Icefield Tools" leading a new standard of sophistication in borehole survey technology. Erik continues to push the boundaries of science to create tools that are forever more versatile and accurate. Still at the company's helm, he hires people who bring the same passion, innovation and purpose to their work, and who like

Box 6.6. **Collaboration among Industry, Accademia and Governments to develop cold climate technology** *(cont.)*

him, are as dedicated to creating great tools as they are to supporting their customers in reaping all the benefits in the field.

Research and business development support have been a critical part of the success story. Cold Climate Innovation (CCI) of the Yukon Research Centre at Yukon College partnered with Icefield Tools, to further advance borehole drilling technology. This partnership developed technology and software that support the mining, oil and gas industries, providing real time data for greater drilling accuracy while significantly reducing overall survey time and associated costs.

The Yukon Business Development Project (YBDP) is an innovative and efficient programme to provide advice, coaching and other services to selected Yukon businesses including technology-based companies, giving them the knowledge and resources to develop to the next level of commercial success and the opportunity to become export capable. This Project carried out by the Whitehorse Chamber of Commerce, the Yukon Technology Innovation Centre, the Yukon Government, INAC, CanNor and the National Research Council selected local technology-based Yukon companies which had high expansion potential and provided to those companies with the human resources and business counsel they needed to help them to reach their full market potential.

YBDP provided Icefield Tools with assistance in the development of business and marketing plans and significantly, with business advisory boards tailored to their individual needs. These boards, consist of local and out-of-territory domain experts, that provide the client companies with the expertise they need to overcome obstacles and promote the rational growth of their operations and market potential. Icefield underwent a period of mentorship and development lasting approximately about one year. During this period, the Business Advisor and Project Manager audited, advised and coached the company and helped them to implement the recommendations of the Business Advisory Board. Icefield Tools has become a nimble team of specialists and global leaders in the field of precision borehole survey technology. An educated labour force, a government-supported research centre at Yukon College and targeted business development have all contributed to Yukon's sucess.

Yukon has been an active contributor to world cold climate technologies, developing expertise that has contributed to the development of ice-field drills for NASA and a remote airstrip in Antarctica. As resources become scarce and eyes turn to more remote locations such as the Arctic, Yukon will be a role model with its research and development teams leading the way.

The Research Centre is housed at Yukon College. Cold Climate Innovation (CCI) is focused on the development, commercialisation and export of sustainable cold climate technologies and related solutions for subarctic regions around the world. CCI supports the partnership between applied scientific researchers, industry and government dedicated to addressing cold climate issues affecting northerners. CCI project areas include alternative energy, building construction, climate-related research, environmental remediation, food security and mechanical innovation.

Work with employers on assuring decent work and skills utilisation

Skills utilisation approaches look at how the workforce is structured and the relationship between an individual's skills and the needs of business. Skills utilisation approaches focus on how well employers are utilising the skills of their employees, which can improve productivity and profitability. Individuals also gain from the better utilisation of their skills through greater job satisfaction and autonomy. This approach avoids supply-side or "provider driven" training solutions, which may not address the breadth of an enterprise's organisational context. Instead, providers are encouraged to take on a workforce development role (Froy, Giguère and Meghnagi, 2012).

In 2013 the federal government announced changes to its Labour Market Development Agreements. At the same time the Government in conjunction with the Provinces and Territories announced a new Canada Job Grant designed to help employers train new or existing employees for jobs that need to be filled. This flexible programme is designed to meet the needs of businesses of all sizes, in all industries and regions. The scheme requires matching funds from employers as well as provinces and territories. Businesses with a plan to train Canadians for an existing job or a better job are eligible to apply for a Canada Job Grant. The Grant provides access to a maximum CAD 5 000 federal contribution per person towards training at eligible training institutions. This means the Grant could provide CAD 15 000 or more per person, including provincial/territorial and employer contributions.

Saskatchewan

Similar to findings under OECD LEED's Leveraging Training and Skills Development in SMEs study in Canada, Saskatchewan recognises the importance of increasing demand for training in SMEs, which are a vital employer base for competitiveness (Bélanger and Hart, 2012). There are two dimensions of the province's efforts. The skills and training centres in Regina and Saskatoon organise their course offerings, develop their course content and deliver training in conjunction with local employers. Employers who work with the centres have the first chance to hire graduates. A number of policies create obligations for companies to hire indigenous workers. Organisations like SIIT and Saskatchewan Polytechnic work with employers to match training to the firms' requirements. Whitecap forms formal partnerships with companies that include skill development components. However, like in many other places, smaller firms have developed a habit of relying on responsive employment services and colleges to provide them with the desired workforce. A tight labour market has tended to keep the system responsive.

The Canada-Saskatchewan Job Grant is the mechanism used in Saskatchewan to support alignment of training with skills needed by employers. Through this programme, employers and government will partner to fund training for unemployed or underemployed individuals leading to a new or better full-time job. The Canada-Saskatchewan Job Grant is open to businesses and non-profit organisations in Saskatchewan. Training must result in a new hire, or a better job. The grant supports new investments in training and is not intended to replace an employer's existing investment in training.

Yukon

The situation in Yukon is somewhat unique. A very large share of the economy is in the public administration. Outside of mining, there are relatively few large firms. Yukon has focused significant attention on working with the 14 First Nation communities to build governance and leadership capability to ensure strong self-government. The other policy directly related to skills utilization is found in the Territory's economic development policy. This translates into connections with Yukon College in the selection of courses and development of curriculum.

The Federal Government under Skills and Partnership Fund (SPF) looks at improving indigenous labour market outcomes through skills development and training, and investments in opportunity-driven projects focused on training for specific job vacancies in high demand sectors. In Yukon, the Yukon Mine training Association (YMTA) works with the industry and First Nations to offer workshops, life and career coaching and specific skills development training to increase the numbers of indigenous people who choose mining as a career. First Nations are also developing programmes through their education and employment services to create opportunities for local First Nations citizens to have greater access to jobs created through self-government.

The Canada-Yukon job Grant launched in September 2014, and is directed by individual employers and organisations acting on behalf of employers (e.g. employer consortia, union halls, industry associations and training coordinators) in the private and not-for-profit sectors. First Nation Governments and selected crown corporations are also eligible recipients.

Promotion of skills for entrepreneurship

Saskatchewan

Saskatchewan Polytechnic offers programmes in entrepreneurship ranging from discovering entrepreneurship to full 32 week programmes in Entrepreneurship and Small Business (Saskatchewan Polytechnic, 2014). A significant focus is placed around supporting individuals in trades programmes who may wish to start their own company. Clients who are eligible for Employment Insurance have access to the Self-Employment Programme, which provides unemployed people with income and entrepreneurial support while they develop and start their business. Successful applicants experience intensive business skills development training while completing a comprehensive business plan that fully supports their business idea. In addition, participants are provided with on-going business advisor counselling services and income support for up to 42 weeks while they develop and implement their business plan.

The Canadian Federation of Independent Business (CFIB) has rated Regina as a top tier entrepreneurial city. The Chamber of Commerce provides useful guidance for those starting a business as well as on-going support and mentorship. RROC has a Business Resource Development Centre to help promote new businesses. The business ecosystem approach employed by RROC sees smaller local business providing services to larger enterprises as a way of capturing as much possible value for the local area. Whitecap looks to build a business ecosystem including locally developed start-ups. To date these are mostly trade and service businesses that serve the First Nation and its larger business ventures.

Yukon

Yukon has a small but vibrant business community focused on providing goods and services to Yukoners and supporting the mining, energy and infrastructure developments in the Territory. Yukon College has developed a number of courses to support entrepreneurship (Yukon College, 2012). Introduction to Entrepreneurship is designed to assist students with determining what they need to build a successful private business. In addition to supporting students in their effort to expand upon their ideas and develop a roadmap for their business career, the course is also designed to provide mentorship opportunities to participants.

Yukon Upstarts, a not-for-profit, runs conferences and seminars to promote entrepreneurship in the territory. In early May 2015 Yukon Upstarts held a three-day programme in Whitehorse. Because of the small business community in the territory, there is also a view that more needs to be done. The CFIB has been calling for a vision for entrepreneurship in the Territory that includes a focus on solutions to labour shortages, competitive taxation, reducing the red tape burden and improving the overall costs of doing business in Yukon.

Entrepreneurship is an important feature of First Nations Development. Specific numbers are not available for Yukon but the Business Development Bank of Canada reports that there has been a 30% increase since the 1996-2001 period (BDC, 2015). Toronto Dominion Bank notes that indigenous small business is growing at a rate that is six times faster than in the non- indigenous market and that indigenous entrepreneurs tend to be about 10 years younger than non- indigenous entrepreneurs.

Tourism and providing the wide variety of services needed by self-governing First Nations offer extensive opportunities. In 2009, the International Centre for Governance and Development provided a comprehensive overview of the existing drivers and barriers of entrepreneurship in the north and argued that Northern entrepreneurs must be supported in order to capitalise on advantages unique to the north, which include: limited competition; the chance to provide essential services to communities; a rich and active cultural heritage; and economic spin-off opportunities from the strong government presence.

The paper concluded that: the conditions in the north and the issues facing the north are ripe for entrepreneurism; the challenges facing entrepreneurs are unique when compared to their southern counterparts; Northern entrepreneurship shares much in common with social and environmental entrepreneurism; the promotion of entrepreneurism must involve local communities if it is to be successful (Buckler et al., 2009).

Economic development promotes quality jobs for local people

Saskatchewan

The Saskatchewan Plan for Growth establishes the goal of creating an additional 60 000 jobs by 2020. The focus of that job growth is in the non-renewable resource extraction business; agriculture and food related businesses; as well as investments in public infrastructure. These are all sectors where there are plentiful good paying jobs. The challenge for Saskatchewan is seen as ensuring the necessary supply of skills to support the pace of growth expected in the province. While there has been some slowing of the rate of growth in recent months, the provinces diversified economy has tempered the impact of falling energy prices.

Planning for Saskatchewan's postsecondary sector is driven from the plan for growth, as are the skills development activities for the trades. In fact, the province sees a requirement to increase the cap on provincial immigrant nominees from 4 000 to 6 000. Specific attention in the Plan for Growth is paid to increasing the participation of indigenous in the economy in part as a way of remedying the historic lower participation rates of Saskatchewan's First Nation and Métis peoples and in part reaching out to the most rapidly growing segment of the provinces population. The Saskatchewan Government has set goals to reduce the disparity between indigenous graduation rates with those of non-indigenous people. Whitecap is an example of where this can make a difference (see Box 6.7).

Box 6.7. **First Nation Economic Development**

Whitecap Dakota First Nation has been a leader in economic development and has created jobs for its members as well as employment opportunities for people in neighbouring communities. Much of what has contributed to the community's economic success was the inclusion of Whitecap under the First Nations Land Management Regime and developing the Whitecap Land Code. Controlling its own land the Chief and Council created an integrated land use plan, established relations with financial institutions to gain access to capital and created long term lease arrangements that allowed companies to establish operations in the community. Whitecap Dakota First Nation has zoned 1 000 acres of reserve lands for commercial development. The resulting business development has created long term revenue streams for the Whitecap government including land leases, property taxes, consumption taxes and utility payments

The Chief and Council recognised that increasing wealth and opportunity for the community and securing future prosperity would require making investments that would deliver economic benefits over the long term. They made that vision a reality by incorporating the Whitecap Development Corporation in 1990. The Whitecap Development Corporation is solely owned by the Whitecap Dakota First Nation but since its inception has put a strong emphasis on developing partnerships that bring the right combination of skill and experience for successful investments. The Corporation has used this strategy to complete several major projects that continue to produce financial benefits for partners and substantial economic growth within the Whitecap Community.

Current business investments have focused on two main streams. The Dakota Hospitality strategy is developing a destination resort that includes Dakota Dunes Golf Links, Dakota Dunes Casino, Tatanka Bison Ranch, Whitecap Trail Gas Plus and proposes the development of Dakota Dunes Hotel and residential resort. The Whitecap Industrial strategy includes six partnerships under the Whitecap Industrial Services Group, Whitecap Commercial Real Estate, and proposes the development of a light industrial business park.

The Development Corporation various activities have resulted in the employment of some 600 people, most in the hospitality and tourism sectors. Hiring is starting to diversify to other sectors such as manufacturing, and employment opportunities are offered beyond the immediate community with recruitment for some positions being province-wide to find employees with the skills they need. Approximately 500 employees commute to Whitecap each day from outside the community. Whitecap has become a major economic player in the region making positive contributions to Saskatchewan's economy.

The federal government has a programme of funding for indigenous people. Under the Procurement Strategy for Aboriginal Business (PSAB), qualified indigenous firms can bid on government procurement contracts through several business arrangements, such as sub-contracting and joint ventures with other firms. The PSAB is open to all indigenous businesses, including sole proprietorship, limited companies, co-operatives, partnerships, and not-for-profit organisations. Since PSAB's establishment in 1996, more than 100 000 contracts have been awarded to indigenous suppliers with a total value of CAD 3.3 billion.

Yukon

Economic development strategy in Yukon is outlined in Pathways to Prosperity. It outlines Yukon's key endowments as its natural wealth both in terms of resources but also in its natural beauty and its advantageous location between Alaska and British Columbia.

The strategy is to encourage incoming investments in the natural resources and tourism through focusing on five enabling factors. In practise, the way the inward investment has worked is that companies moving to Yukon bring a lot of the human resources with them. This can range from virtually all personnel in "fly-in, fly-out" mining operations to management resources in other industries. Yukon's strategy is to either get those people to choose to reside in Yukon or to look for opportunities to replace transient labour with locals. In addition Yukon looks to capture a high proportion of jobs in what are termed supporting industries. These are typically small business that directly supply larger players with product and services or benefit from downstream wage expenditures such as retail.

First Nations have their own strategies that are driven through their development corporations and administrations. Tourism has been a target for two of the three case study First Nations with Kwalin Dunn building a large conference facility in the city of Whitehorse and Tr'ondëk Hwëch'in leading efforts to have Dawson City designated as a UNESCO World Heritage site (Canadian Northern Economic Development Agency, 2013; Tr'ondëk Hwëch'in Council, 2013).

Theme 4: Being inclusive

Figure 6.6. **Dashboard results for being inclusive**

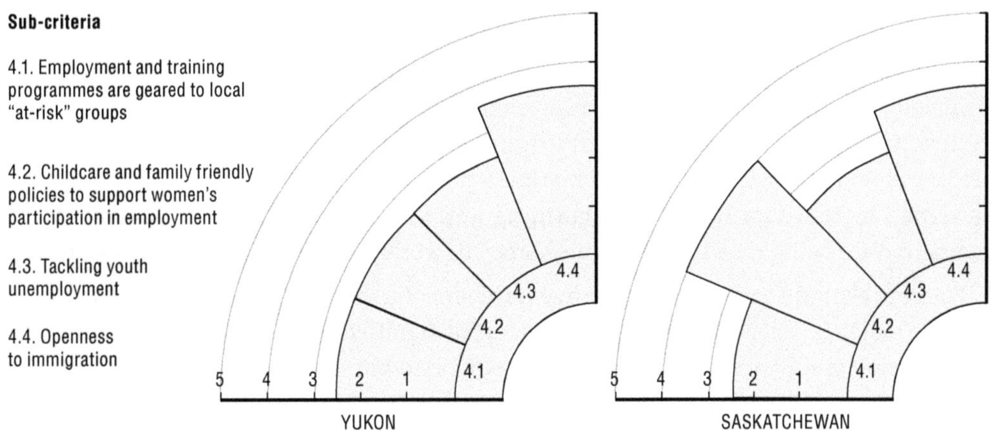

Employment and training programmes are geared to local "at-risk" groups

Saskatchewan

Saskatchewan administers Income Assistance at the provincial level. There are a number of dimensions to the Programme. Saskatchewan Assistance provides for basic needs while Saskatchewan Assured Disability Assistance covers individuals for whom work is not possible. There is also Temporary Assistance (the T-Program) which is provided for those who could find work with the provision of skills or work preparation training. In addition, there are a series of supports and supplements to cover special situations such as the need for childcare or housing.

There are about 2 000 Income Assistance Recipients in the Province – half of which are in the T-Programme. Specific figures were not available for Regina but as the employment rates are quite high there are fewer recipients on the T-Programme and a larger percentage have multiple barriers. During this OECD review, interviewees confirmed that there are an increasing number of their clients who require more intensive interventions over longer periods before becoming work ready.

The Saskatchewan Plan for Growth specifically targets literacy as a key priority to address disadvantage. The Plan calls for an elimination of wait time for adult basic education programmes. There are two other "at risk" groups which include unemployed youth and First Nation/Metis. There are a number of programmes for each of these groups in place in Regina funded through federal contribution agreements; Saskatchewan contribution agreements and community based funding.

It is difficult to assess whether the programme response meets the need as there does not appear to be a good source of base information and there is an absence of planning bodies examining and co-ordinating the various responses on the ground. During this OECD review, interviews did confirm that there is informal co-ordination among the various agencies and that there used to be greater formal organisation among the various players but that there has been a decline in network activity over the last several years.

Because of its small size and administration, Whitecap has a clearer understanding of community members who are "at risk" and takes an individual case management approach for the provision of income assistance and interventions. Whitecap represents a success story of having moved from nearly 90% unemployment in 1990 to rates comparable to the provincial average, and having income assistance levels come down from 100 cases to less than 20.

Yukon

Yukon Health and Social Services administer Income Assistance. There are about 800 non-indigenous individuals receiving income assistance in the territory. A small team at the ministry manages programmes to assist individuals into work. Currently there are about 60 individuals who are receiving support to transition into work. For persons with disabilities there are provisions under the Labour Market Agreement for Persons with Disabilities that was signed in February of 2014. Programing and enhanced services supported by the agreement were being rolled out in Whitehorse but were yet to be initiated in Dawson City.

For First Nations communities, a large numbers of individuals on Income Assistance is a critical challenge. High assistance rates represent significant costs for self-governing First Nations. Employment and training are being expanded but there are structural constraints that make the transition from income assistance to work difficult. These include the same level of income between entry level jobs and the income assistance rate; some jobs such as mining are seen as in conflict with traditional values; and, there remains socio-cultural resistance among some employers to employ indigenous people.

In the Yukon region, the Ta'an Kwach'an Council is working closely in collaboration with the Council of Yukon First Nations to deliver the Income Assiststance Reform in the Whitehorse catchment area. Through the Enhanced Service Delivery, the Ta'an Kwach'an Council provides eligible Income Assistance recipients, aged 18-24, access to a range of services and programmes, aimed at increasing their employability and guiding and supporting them as they move into the workforce. The First Nations Job Fund is delivered through the Council of Yukon First Nations and provides jobs and skills training needed to support recipients in securing employment.

Childcare and family friendly policies to support women's participation in employment

Administered through the Aboriginal Skills and Employment Training Strategy, the First Nations and Inuit Child Care Initiative aims to increase the supply of quality childcare services in First Nations and Inuit communities to a level comparable to the general population in communities (The Muttart Foundation, 2013). Through the First Nations and Inuit Childcare Initiative, participating Aboriginal Skills and Employment Training Strategy Agreement Holders transfer funding to child care centres in order to support culturally appropriate child care spaces in First Nations and Inuit Communities. In Saskatchewan, the Saskatchewan Indian Training Assessment Group receives FNICCI funding. In the Yukon, both the Aboriginal Labour Force Alliance and the Council of Yukon First Nations receive FNICCI funding.

Saskatchewan

One in five Saskatchewan families have children five years of age and under (79 470 children in the province under 6 years of age). Between the 2006-11 census, the number of children aged 4 and under grew by close to 20% and the province's fertility rate reached 2.06; the highest among Canada's provinces.

Saskatchewan has a complex mixture of policies around childcare. In 1996, for example, the province introduced publicly funded prekindergarten for vulnerable children. In 2000, it implemented operating grants for child care services. In 2004, it moved to a regional delivery model and increased the educational requirements for early childhood educators. In 2006, Saskatchewan was the first province to move regulated child care into the education department (then Saskatchewan Learning).

The province has favoured not-for-profit provision of childcare through targeting its programmes of subsidies to non-profit centres. Cost is affordable based on a generous subsidy structure however availability can be a problem. About 48% of families in the province (just above the overall national use level) employed childcare services. Female participation rates in Saskatchewan were 63.6%, above the national average of 61.6% (Statistics Canada, 2014). Female participation rates are in some measure a reflection of the availability of childcare and other child friendly work policies. In Regina, the rate is slightly higher at 64.2%.

Yukon

Yukon Health and Social Services, Child Care Services delivers 7 service programmes designed to help individual families and licensed child care facilities. These services include childcare subsidies and direct operating grants to licensed child facilities. The unit provides administrative, consultative and support services, and licenses child care facilities to ensure they follow legislated standards (Government of Yukon, 2014).

The Child Care Subsidy Programme assists families who need childcare for their children and may not be able to afford the cost of child care. The amount of subsidy is based on an income test, which is the combined net income of the family. This test takes into account family size, income, and the community in which the family lives. In recent years, high rates of childbirths in Whitehorse have put pressure on local childcare providers a number of whom were operating at capacity. Dawson City suffers a similar problem. Dawson City's only public daycare has just 20 spaces and a waiting list of as many kids.

The participation rate among women is quite high at 77.1% in Whitehorse (NHS, 2011). This is in part because of the large share of Yukon's economy that resides in the Public Sector that has historically higher rates of female employment and a higher level of professional jobs that allow for families to pay for privately provided childcare. Yukon is focused on engaging all segments of the society including business to promote a strong wellness oriented society that includes workplace balance that allows for family. On The Path Together: Wellness plan for Yukon's Children and Families (2014) is the comprehensive plan that guides government actions in this area.

Box 6.8. **Focusing on the early years in the Yukon**

Having a good education is increasingly a necessary foundation for success in the labour market. Historically primary and secondary schooling has been the responsibility of the Department of Indigenous and Northern Affairs. In the early 1990's an Umbrella Final Agreement was developed for Yukon First nations to become self-governing. By 2005, 11 of Yukon's 14 First Nations were self-governing.

As each First Nation reached their Final Agreement, they also signed a Self-Government Agreement (SGA). The agreements provide for funding which support the delivery of programmes and services at the First Nation level. Under the SGA the First Nation has the power to make and enact laws in respect of their lands and citizens, to tax, to provide for municipal planning, and to manage or co-manage lands and resources. Each self-governing First Nation has a constitution that contains the membership code, establishes governing bodies and provides for its powers, and protects the rights and freedoms of its citizens. As self-governing bodies, First Nations are not precluded from asserting any of the rights of any Canadian citizen or corporation. Each Yukon First Nation also has the power to make laws with respect to the provision of training and the provision of education programmes and services for its citizens.

In 2013, 9 of the 14 Yukon First Nations signed a Memorandum of Understanding (MOU) with the Government of Canada, and the Yukon. The context of this MOU differs from other education agreements in Canada, as there are no band operated schools in the Yukon (all First Nation students attend schools operated by the Territorial Government). The benefits of being part of the greater system are similar to those outlined for Whitecap Dakota. The MOU establishes a partnership in education between the three parties and commit to creating and implementing a joint action plan, for the success of First Nations' learners. Provisions are made within the MOU to recognize the diversity of Yukon First Nation peoples, communities, language, culture, traditions and spiritual practices and the need for culturally-appropriate education.

At the same time the Council of Yukon First Nations established First Nations Education Commission (FNEC) to provide technical support, advice and recommendations to Yukon First Nations that are members of FNEC with respect to education matters relating to Yukon First Nation citizens and communities. These education matters include early childhood education, primary and secondary education and employment training. The Commission works toward common and unified strategies and recommendations aimed at advancing YFN education; improving student learning outcomes for YFN students and improving the involvement and engagement of YFN students, parents, families and communities in the school system.

There still remain significant differences between First Nations and non-First Nations in Graduation rates. The graduation rate for Non First Nations is 79% in Yukon and 48% for First Nations. The Yukon first nations Education Action Plan 2014-2024 sets eliminating this difference as a high priority. The areas of priority state "Closing the academic achievement gap between First Nations students and non-First Nations students in Yukon and in Canada is a long-standing priority for First Nations people throughout the country. It is a priority for Yukon First Nations that Yukon First Nations students attain and exceed academic requirements. It is widely understood that eliminating the education gap will contribute positively to the social, economic, cultural and political landscape of the Yukon and Canada.

Box 6.8. **Focusing on the early years in the Yukon** *(cont.)*

Their remains considerable work to do to bring the First Nations graduation rate up to that of Non First Nations Yukoners but as one senior Education official put it there is a significant incentive for the Territorial Government as First Nations could, if dissatisfied with the progress create their own school system.

Tackling youth unemployment

Saskatchewan

Saskatchewan's youth unemployment rate has been creeping up over the last twelve months from 9.2% in May 2014 to 11.7% in May 2015. This is slightly faster than the increase in unemployment for those over 25. When examined by gender the rate for young women in nearly twice that of young men (men 8.3%, women 15.5% [Labour force survey estimates, table 282-0003]). In May 2015, Regina recorded a slightly higher rate of youth unemployment than the rest of the province at 13.1% (Labour force survey estimates, table 282-0128). For Indigenous youth, the unemployment rate in Regina reached 25.3% in the same period.

Saskatchewan does not have a separate strategy for youth unemployment. Efforts have been directed at providing multiple pathways to higher education and in particular making it easy for young people to enter the trades. Labour Market Services have counsellors to provide assistance to those unfamiliar with the labour market. In addition the Rainbow Youth Centre and First Nations Employment Centre offer services tailored to youth.

Yukon

Whitehorse has a Youth Employment Centre-Skookum Jim that has the objective to help youth develop the necessary skills to successfully gain and maintain meaningful employment. The Centre works on assisting youth who struggle with employment through tailored support and training on an individual basis. Programmes are divided into general services that include Job search tools and resources; drop-in Centre with access to computer lab, fax machine, photo copier, phone; and career development workshops (resume & cover letter writing, interview prep, job search strategies).

Special services are available for those who have not completed high school. Services for this group include: meaningful paid 3 month work placements; life skills training (First Aid, How To Stretch Your Money, WHIMIS); and case management with onsite youth employment coordinators.

4.4. *Openness to immigration*

Saskatchewan

Immigration plays an important role in the labour market development strategy for the province. The Plan for Growth calls for an increase in the population of the province by 60 000 people with a significant portion of that coming from immigration. The province wishes to increase the cap on the provincial nominee programme (the part of the federal immigration programme where provinces identify immigration requirements to the specific labour market needs of the province) by 50% from 4 000 to 6 000 per annum.

In Regina immigrants represent about 7% of the city's population slightly higher than the province as a whole (5%) but lower than that of Canada which is 18%. The immigrant share of Regina's population has declined between 1986 and 2001. Immigrants represented 9% of Regina's population in 1986, 8% in 1996 and 7% in 2001. Saskatchewan's immigrant population has remained at 5% since 1996, a decrease from 7% in 1986. The proportion of immigrants in the population of both Regina and Saskatchewan is well below that of Canada which has increased from 16% to 18% over this same period. While the relative share has decreased the absolute numbers while declining modestly in recent years remain at about 3 000 per annum (RROC).

Regina Region Local Immigration Partnership (RRLIP) is a Citizenship and Immigration Canada funded initiative. This community based initiative assesses current community resources and services for newcomers as well as identifies local priorities from extensive consultation with newcomers and the general community. The RRLIP works to facilitate closer collaboration, co-ordinate activities, create efficiencies and build capacity in Regina. The RRLIP is a new structure having been started in April of 2014.

The Regina Open Door Society (RODS) is a non-profit organisation that provides settlement and integration services to refugees and immigrants in Regina. RODS is committed to meeting the needs of newcomers by offering programmes and services that enable them to achieve their goals and participate fully in the larger community.

Yukon

The Government of Yukon administers immigration programmes in partnership with Citizenship and Immigration Canada. This partnership allows Yukon to nominate qualified foreign nationals to the federal government for permanent residency.

The Yukon Nominee Program (YNP) is run by the Yukon Government in partnership with Citizenship and Immigration Canada under the "Agreement for Canada-Yukon Cooperation on Immigration." The YNP streams for Skilled Workers and Critical Impact Workers is locally driven and based on the needs of Yukon employers. When eligible Yukon employers cannot find Canadian citizens or permanent residents to fill permanent full-time jobs, they can find workers from outside of Canada. They select internationally trained and experienced foreign workers who have the skills needed in the local labour market, and nominate them to receive Canadian permanent resident visas to settle and work in Yukon.

In Whitehorse the Multicultural Centre of the Yukon welcomes immigrants to Canada and to the Yukon. Services are available to assist in the settlement and integration of immigrants and refugees into the social, economic, cultural, and political life of their community. Programmes offered are in the areas of settlement services, language instruction, employment services, and community networking.

The total immigrant population in Yukon is small about 4% of the total population, and concentrated primarily in Whitehorse. An important part of this community are Filipinos who are about one quarter of immigrants and supply an important part of labour to local Whitehorse big box retailers and fast food franchises.

During interviews conducted for this OECD review, there was anecdotal evidence that there may be some crowding out occurring in entry-level jobs between foreign workers and other groups trying to access the labour market in particular younger workers and individuals transitioning from income assistance to work. Employers have a preference for the stability that foreign workers offer and the reduced payroll costs associated with foreign workers. Recent changes to the temporary foreign worker programme are seen as putting considerable pressure on employers in Whitehorse who have seen foreign workers as essential to running their business. Local groups and some citizens view the extensive use of foreign workers by some employers as removing an important source of jobs for entry level workers that were available in the community in previous periods.

References

BDC (2015), "Aboriginal entrepreneur", Business Development Bank of Canada, *www.bdc.ca/EN/i_am/aboriginal_entrepreneur/Pages/default.aspx*

Bélanger, P. and S. Hart (2012), "Leveraging Training and Skills Development in SMEs: An Analysis of Two Canadian Urban Regions – Montreal and Winnipeg", *OECD Local Economic and Employment Development (LEED) Working Papers*, No. 2012/19, OECD Publishing, Paris, *http://dx.doi.org/10.1787/5k8x6l198524-en*.

Buckler et al. (2009), "The Northern Entrepreneurship Workshop Proceedings and Report: Fostering entrepreneurship in the North, International Centre for Northern Governance and Development", University of Saskatchewan.

Canadian Northern Economic Development Agency (2013), "Initiatives in Dawson City build capacity and economic activity", CanNor-13-021, Government of Canada, *www.cannor.gc.ca/eng/1385565084906/1385565161912*.

City of Regina (2013), "Design Regina, Official Community Plan", Schedule "A" to Bylaw No. 2013-48, *www.designregina.ca/wp-content/uploads/DesignRegina-TOC.pdf*.

City of Whitehorse (2015), "Community Economic Development Strategy: 2015 to 2020 Work Plan", *www.city.whitehorse.yk.ca/home/showdocument?id=5198*.

Saskatchewan Polytechnic (2014), "Annual Report", *http://saskpolytech.ca/about/about-us/reports-and-statistics/documents/annual-report/annual-report-2014-15.pdf*.

The Muttart Foundation (2013), "Children and Families in New Saskatchewan: A Discussion of Early Learning and Child Care", Edmonton, *www.muttart.org/wp-content/uploads/2013/11/Children-and-Families-in-the-New-Saskatchewan-112013.pdf*.

Tr'ondëk Hwëch'in Council (2014), "Resolution 2014-11-27-04 Apprenticeship Framework".

Tr'ondëk Hwëch'in Council (2013), "Resolution 2013-07-11-01, World heritage Project Committees", *http://tkwhstatus.ca/wp-content/uploads/2013/08/2013_07_11-TH-Council-Resolution.pdf*.

The City of Dawson and Tr'ondëk Hwëch'in (2007), "After the Gold Rush: The integrated sustainable Community Development Plan", *www.infrastructure.gov.yk.ca/pdf/icsp_dawson.pdf*.

Yukon College (2012), "First Nations Leadership Training", Whitehorse, *https://yukoncollege.yk.ca/programs/info/fnlt*.

Yukon College (2011), "First Nations Governance and Public Administration Brochure", Whitehorse, *www.eco.gov.yk.ca/aboriginalrelations/pdf/fngpa_brochure.pdf*.

Chapter 7

Towards an action plan for jobs: Recommendations for better supporting local employment and economic development

Stimulating job creation at the local level requires integrated actions across employment, training, and economic development portfolios. Co-ordinated place based policies can help workers find suitable jobs, while also contributing to demand by stimulating productivity. This requires flexible policy management frameworks, information, and integrated partnerships which leverage the efforts of local stakeholders. This chapter outlines the key recommendations emerging from the review of local job creation policies in Canada, including Saskatchewan and the Yukon.

Recommendations for local employment and economic development of indigenous communities

This OECD review has looked at employment, skills, and economic development issues in the Yukon and Saskatchewan across four case study areas, which include Dawson City, Whitehorse, Whitecap First Nations and Regina. Relative to other jurisdictions in Canada, Saskatchewan and the Yukon have relatively low unemployment rates and a significant prevalence of employers reporting skills shortages, particularly in the resources sector.

With a focus on indigenous communities, the study has provided an opportunity to look at different governance models for First Nations and the interactions of local self-government administrative practices with surrounding municipal administrations, provincial/territorial authorities and the federal government. Both Saskatchewan and the Yukon have a significant number of indigenous communities, which face particular barriers to participation and labour market success.

In Canada, self-government agreements empower an indigenous community to govern in a manner that is responsive to the needs and interests of its people. While there are no self-government agreements currently in place in Saskatchewan, in the Yukon, they are changing the face of First Nations governance and altering the relationship between First Nations, the Yukon government, and the federal government. These agreements enable First Nations to change a long-standing narrative of deprivation and exclusion to one of inclusive growth, employment and prosperity.

Greater economic and social outcomes activities can be achieved by indigenous communities through stronger policy enablers and capacity building activities. This OECD review has demonstrated the interests of indigenous communities to lead employment and economic development activities in their community in collaboration with the resources, covenants and practices in the municipal jurisdiction(s) adjacent to the community, as well as the departments (ministries) implicated at the territorial and provincial level.

The following recommendations should be considered to boost employment and economic development activities within indigenous communities in Canada.

Recommendation: Recognise that provincial and territorial governments are playing an increasingly active role in indigenous communities and have considerable incentives to ensure successful economic and social development. This may well involve rethinking the federal leadership role in areas where provinces and territories have strong capacity and competence.

Where possible, the federal government should award more flexibility to its local and regional offices to work with provincial/territorial employment and income assistance programmes so they can better align services in the broader community with those offered in indigenous communities. It is critical to establish a local lens when developing policies and programmes for employment, training, and economic development (OECD, 2014a). At the local level, strategic initiatives to build resiliency, and achieve high employment can do much to change the economic and social future of a community.

Flexibility within social assistance policies is a key issue for indigenous communities as there are funding policy incentives within the system to keep individuals on social assistance rather than encourage integration into the labour market. The federal government should provide incentives to the provincial/territorial level to take a stronger role in coordinating services for First Nations, including those under federal responsibility. Currently, co-ordination and flexibility are problematic in part because some of the services are managed at federal and provincial government levels and do not effectively promote linkages with other programmes and activities locally.

Many of the current policy and programmes are designed in a centralised and specialised manner, which assumes that indigenous communities are separated from a broader social and economic environment and that indigenous people only access specialised services developed for their communities. The policy environment is considerably more complex and in some cases, First Nations communities may wish to align or in some cases integrate their services with those of the surrounding area to obtain efficiencies or to make them more effective. There could be advantages to be gained from policy integration by establishing locally based employment and economic development boards in some communities to formalise partnership working and better integrate activities as well as the involvement of employers. In areas where there are significant self-governing indigenous communities, the board should combine or co-ordinate services across communities.

In both Saskatchewan (Whitecap Dakota First Nation) and the Yukon, First Nation students are being taught by local school boards. These unique approaches have advantages in terms of teacher's professional development and support, standards of schools and quality of curriculum while respecting the cultural integrity of First Nations education. For indigenous youth, closer integration appears to ease important transitions from primary school to high school and from high school to postsecondary education. The successful pre-K to 12 integration of Whitecap with the Saskatoon Public School Division provides a model that may be applicable in other First Nations communities across Canada. Critical to that success was the willingness of Whitecap Dakota First Nation, the Saskatoon School Board, and the federal government to work together to implement an arrangement that would improve student outcomes.

To take advantage of a changing policy landscape at the provincial/territorial level and to increase the ability of communities to organise activities that best respond to local needs, the federal government should seek to develop more indigenous policies and programmes jointly with the provinces/territories. Furthermore, where responsibilities cannot be devolved directly to the community level, the federal government should ensure that local representatives have the ability to work with community leaders and provincial/territorial authorities to affect action. This would mean that federal departments should review their programme procedures with a view to confer increased decisional authority to policy officers who reside in the local communities. Local federal officials are active in local economic and labour mechanisms where they exist and the federal contribution is appreciated. Intergovernmental co-ordination is becoming increasingly important to develop effective strategies to boost indigenous labour market and economic development.

Recommendation: Strategically use public procurement policies to add conditions on contracts around the employment of indigenous individuals and/or to increase the number of apprenticeship and training opportunities.

Canada has established important mechanisms to promote indigenous enterprise development through programmes both at the federal and provincial/territorial levels. During this OECD review, some promising examples were observed in the creation of specific indigenous and business partnerships but the majority of programmes and strategies do not include reference to job creation within the indigenous community itself. There is the possibility of more precise targeting of these programmes to direct the benefits towards local economic development and job creation and develop specific skills (e.g. literacy, numeracy) and apprenticeships within First Nation communities.

Some functions currently performed by the provincial or territorial government can be rethought in such a way as to create employment. In Yukon, officials at Community Services are reviewing delivery to see what services could be provided locally in the community. In Saskatchewan provision of policing, medical and day care services are being thought of for the surrounding region to give critical mass to facilities located on the Whitecap Dakota First Nation. Each innovation while small in itself has the effect of building community capacity and strengthening the local economy.

Public procurement also represents an important policy lever the government has at its disposal to promote job creation within indigenous communities. While some programmes exist, more needs to be done to ensure indigenous communities benefit from these funding arrangements in a manner, which promotes economic development within their community. Preferential treatment can be given to First Nation-owned businesses (e.g., either through set-asides or awarding additional points to First Nation-owned businesses in the bid process) while on the supply side, additional capacity building and outreach programmes which go further than providing information can help First Nations businesses in developing the capacities needed to win and deliver on government contracts. Incentivising other large government contractors to sub-contract with First Nation-owned businesses is another way to increase access to public procurement while also building the capacities of First Nation businesses to eventually become prime contractors.

Public procurement contracts can also be structured in such a way as to improve access to employment opportunities and training for First Nations people outside of First Nations owned businesses. Conditions can be put into public procurement contracts requiring that a certain number of employment or apprenticeship opportunities be awarded to First Nations people, or extra points in the bid process can be awarded to contractors with strategies in place to promote First Nations employment and training. Similar levers can be used via local planning decisions – for example, through conditioning planning approval on offering a certain number of employment or training opportunities.

Recommendation: Strengthen leadership capacities and facilitate information sharing to enable identification of the most promising conditions for success across Canada's indigenous communities by establishing a repository of effective practices in promoting indigenous employment and skills development activities

The federal government should play a stronger role in sharing information across indigenous communities and building leadership capacities. This is particularly important for those First Nations communities, who have successfully concluded self-government agreements. This report has highlighted the efforts within the Yukon to develop local leadership, governance and public administration capacities through the First Nations Leadership training programmes delivered by Yukon College. This programme model is an interesting practice, which could be adapted in other communities across Canada. Greater information sharing could take the form of a "centre for excellence" – a constantly evolving repository of experience and best practices in managing change and establishing sound, transparent and accountable governance frameworks across over 600 First Nations communities in Canada. The concept of a "centre for excellence" has received support from indigenous groups, such as the National Aboriginal Economic Development Board.

Towards an action plan for jobs: Recommendations for Saskatchewan

This study has looked at the range of institutions and actors in Saskatchewan with a particular focus on local activities in Whitecap and Regina. A number of strengths and challenges were observed which should be considered to further promote job creation and skills development in Saskatchewan.

Recommendation: Promote stronger local employment and economic development networks and inject greater flexibility into the management and implementation of policies at the local level

The Saskatchewan Plan for Growth establishes the goal of creating an additional 60 000 jobs by 2020. The focus of the plan is through job growth in the non-renewable resource sector; agriculture and food related businesses; as well as investments in public infrastructure. The Plan for Growth has been effective in focusing and co-ordinating the efforts of various Ministries by providing an integrated approach and promoting better cross ministry policy co-ordination. However, formal governance arrangements to co-ordinate the work of various employment and economic development organisations at the local level appear weak. Mechanisms that naturally link municipalities to local labour market activity are not optimal. For example, social assistance and vocational education are administered provincially, whereas economic development is driven out of a stand-alone administration locally. In the area of employment services, there are an increasing number of organisations that offer what appear to be similar services to urban First Nations.

During this review, local employment service providers in Regina highlighted that more flexibility in the design and delivery of services would ensure they are able to adequately cater services to particular client groups. Local employment services face a changing client profile resulting from the increase in the number of individuals who face multiple barriers to enter employment, larger caseloads of people on income assistance, and increased numbers of indigenous moving into the city and looking for work. More flexibility would be to enable service providers to have a stronger role in negotiating programme design criteria such as the intensity of the intervention (e.g. how long a client is able to be served) as well as setting and/or negotiating performance targets which take into account local employment conditions.

In Regina, there was limited interaction among the various actors involved in economic, employment and skills development. No formal mechanism exists that connects labour force planning and skills development strategies with the economic development plans for the region. The co-ordination between Service Canada and provincial programmes also needs to be strengthened. Job seekers would benefit from greater co-ordination among service providers locally and better information about where to go to receive services.

Previous OECD research highlighted the critical role to be played by local boards in assessing local strengths, weaknesses, threats, opportunities, as well as linking supply and demand approaches to skills and employment, particularly in areas of low-skills equilibrium (OECD, 2014a; Verma, 2012). Saskatchewan should pilot the establishment of a local board in

Regina to promote stronger linkages and co-ordination among the various policy portfolios. The board could bring together key players in the community to align services and agree on strategic objectives for local employment and economic development.

Box 7.1. **Local boards in Ontario and the United States**

Ontario, Canada: there are 25 Workforce Planning Boards who conduct localised research and actively engage organisations and community partners in local labour market projects. Every local workforce planning board publishes detailed reports about its labour market projects, activities and partnerships. Local workforce planning boards champion local workforce development solutions for their communities and help to strategically align the actions of all local stakeholders in the community. Previous OECD research looked at workforce planning boards in Hamilton and Thunder Bay and found that the boards serve useful roles as information nodes and have led to the creation of valuable and strong networks, which are a form of social capital (OECD, 2014b).

United States: Local workforce investment boards (WIBs) have played a strong role in creating more integrated strategies to address employment and skills within broader economic development strategies locally since 1998. There are over 600 WIBs across the United States, at the state and local level, and they are strongly business-led, being both chaired by business and having a majority of business members. Each local workforce investment area is governed by such a board, which is responsible for providing employment and training services within a specific geographic area.

Source: (2014b), *Employment and Skills Strategies in Canada*, OECD Reviews on Local Job Creation, OECD Publishing, Paris; OECD. (2014c), *Employment and Skills Strategies in the United States*, OECD Reviews on Local Job Creation, OECD Publishing, Paris, OECD.

Recommendation: Encourage labour market development stakeholders – including colleges and universities – to become more engaged in accessing, analysing, and producing local labour market information. This includes developing stronger forecasting methods of future skill needs as well as informing students of potential job opportunities

A key part of the policy/implementation cycle is having good information upon which to make decisions. Saskatchewan has relatively small cities and as a result little locally produced information is being used. Better local information would create greater capacity at the local level by providing more information on successful strategies for employment and skills.

Authoritative and updated skills profiles of local labour markets are important in framing strategies and strengthening accountability and can also galvanise local actors into a common agenda for action when used well (OECD, 2014a). The source for a majority of the data used at the local level is the census and the labour force survey (which does not include on-reserve information). For smaller areas, the long form census has been a significant source of data and information that was replaced by the Household Survey in 2011. The federal government recently announced a decision to reinstate the long-form census in 2016 and that will significantly improve the information available for analysis. To ensure robust information and evidence at the local level, new methods and opportunities could be explored to supplement data gathering and analysis in Saskatchewan.

Greater focus also needs to be placed on forecasting future skills needs and anticipating growth opportunities. Saskatchewan could establish a policy process which is focused on future skills planning to ensure that supply is geared towards the future needs of the provincial economy. Any potential establishment of a local board could also play a role in coordinating supply and demand labour market information; however it could also be generated through collaborations among local actors including economic development, the chambers of commerce and the universities and colleges.

Recommendation: Expand the use of demand driven training through stronger linkages with local employers (especially SMEs) and embed skills policies in economic development thinking

In Regina, the Regina Skills and Trades Centre seems to be particularly effective at training and placing participants and is a strong example of a demand driven approach to training in the province. Consideration could be given to expanding it both geographically and in other employment spheres. Working closely with the Regina Chamber of Commerce, it has a board of local business owners. Skills and Trades looks to place all graduates and uses the specific requirements of hiring companies as a way of adding specific employer value around courses that qualify for apprenticeship under the Saskatchewan Apprenticeship and Certification Commission.

Increasing local engagement with employers should occur in an organised manner to minimise the burden on employers and to best use scarce resources. It is important to build on good bottom up collaboration and networks that already exist. In Regina, the Chamber of Commerce has been active in working with Regina Trades and Skills Centre as well as the Regina Regional Opportunities Commission to grow the local economy and the labour force. Local labour market services offices could play a stronger role in convening providers around creating an overall employer engagement strategy.

Going forward, skills policies need to be embedded in a broader drive to support economic development. This can include helping existing firms to move towards more skills intensive, higher value product market strategies. A situation of low-skills equilibrium can develop where there is a concentration of employers in a region that are pursuing price-based competition strategies, and that rely on low-skilled and standardised production. OECD research has shown that local public agencies can contribute to improving how skills are put to use through a number of different policy instruments, such as incentives for employers to invest in new technology and the promotion of more effective forms of work organisation (Froy and Giguère, 2010).

Recent studies have underscored Canada's productivity challenge and potential improvements as they relate to better using skills (Drumond, Caveluck, and Calver, 2015). One such opportunity exists through the implementation of the Canada-Saskatchewan Job Grant. Building the capacity of firms to optimise the utilisation of skills and to make investments in their existing workforce will be essential as part of an overall productivity and innovation strategy in Saskatchewan. Local networks of employers and training institutions could be given a greater policy "steer" to co-ordinate and promote skills utilisation strategies across business in the local area.

For employment services, Saskatchewan could look to the Quebec model where Employment Quebec services are active in offering employers assistance with work organisation and human resources management practices (OECD, 2014a). Given the low unemployment rate in Saskatchewan, there is a stronger opportunity to focus on the existing workforce and how to lift overall productivity.

In many cases, innovation and local economic development can be promoted by boosting skills in traditionally low skill sectors, such as those related to resource development. For example, Saskatchewan polytechnic could play an enhanced role in working with firms in the energy, mineral and manufacturing sectors to improve local skills utilisation and improve productivity through management training and the co-development and dissemination of relevant R&D, product testing and technology transfer. Previous work by the OECD has highlighted the important role that can be played by colleges in fostering synergies between local companies and the educational and research infrastructure to promote skills development and help employers move up the value chain and expand their product offer.

Recommendation: Implement a comprehensive provincial youth employment approach which focuses on employment and job creation as well as smoother transitions into the labour market

When looking at unemployment across Canada, Saskatchewan compares favourably well but this macro-level indicator of economic health masks the challenges faced by certain groups and places in the province. While the youth unemployment rate also compares well across provinces in Canada, it is rising and youth face a number of significant barriers to entering the labour market. There is an opportunity in Saskatchewan to develop a forward looking provincial youth employment strategy, which ensures that youth are given sufficient support to develop the right skills that meet the needs of the labour market.

In thinking about the development of a strategy, Saskatchewan should consider how to enable greater youth ownership within the implementation of programmes and policies. This means looking for ways to directly involve youth in the development and implementation of programmes. Higher-skilled and more ambitious youth can serve as mentors and assist in targeted efforts and outreach, particularly for indigenous youth. Best practices highlight the importance of indigenous mentors, especially for indigenous youth. The province could undertake a strategic review with the goal of looking at existing funding policy mechanisms to ensure that incentives are provided to local service delivery organisations to reduce duplication and join-up efforts. This review would also examine potential actions which could be leveraged at the municipal level.

Addressing barriers to youth unemployment needs to be multi-faceted, especially in regions where multiple service providers co-exist. Outcome-based performance management systems can also have unintended consequences by injecting competition into the delivery of services as providers can be encouraged to cherry pick clients and focus efforts on those individuals most likely to succeed. This OECD study has highlighted the opportunity to co-ordinate services for youth in Regina, where there are a plethora of service providers.

For example, the Glasgow model could be examined for its applicability to larger cities in Saskatchewan, such as Regina and Saskatoon. The city of Glasgow, Scotland has re-engineered its approach to supporting youth employability by shifting support from individual projects to one where the emphasis was placed on improving the entire ecology of interventions available and joining these up. This included establishing clear leadership responsibility, introducing shared targets for the city, establishing a Youth Gateway model to promote information sharing and joint service commissioning, and embedding schools into the partnership model. A number of changes to promote genuine collaboration were also introduced, including establishing a Service Level Agreement in 2009 outlining the roles and responsibilities of all key players and the introduction of youth employability groups to monitor progress on the ground. Under the banner of Glasgow Works, a co-commissioning model was piloted where funders have adopted a more transparent approach to financing interventions.

Towards an action plan for jobs: Recommendations for the Yukon

This study has looked at the range of institutions and actors in the Yukon with a particular focus on local activities in Whitehorse and Dawson City. A number of strengths and challenges were observed which should be considered to further promote job creation and skills in the Yukon.

Recommendation: Build on the success of the Labour Market Framework by establishing local networks in communities in the Yukon that would be tasked with developing employment and economic development plans. These networks should involve employers and be closely connected to the training system

Yukon's labour market activities are driven from the conclusion of a Labour Market Framework agreement, which was initiated in 2008 and combines a far-reaching series of stakeholder committees covering four thematic areas of the territory's labour market strategy, including skills and training; immigration; labour market information; and recruitment and employee retention. The Labour Market Framework appears to be a useful mechanism for seeking local stakeholder input into policy and programme development and is a practice that merits examination by other jurisdictions interested in open policy development. Stakeholders play an active role in informing on-going policy discussions around labour market issues and programme design and implementation. One of the key features of the framework is to look for ways to create greater integration vertically (between different orders of governments), horizontally (among different Ministries in Yukon), as well as between non-governmental delivery organisations, labour representatives and employers.

Yukon is showing leadership in how it is establishing government-to-government relations with self-governing First Nations Communities. Local municipalities and First Nations appear to have strong collaborative working relations. Each First Nation has its own employment and training division as part of its administration. Services are loosely connected to those offered through the Yukon government and citizens can choose to use general services or those specifically connected to the First Nation administration. Services tend to be highly integrated and may involve tight co-operation between the First Nation development corporation and the employment and training division.

Local areas in Yukon have the dual challenge of building a resilient economy less dependent on public investments while also ensuring access to the labour market for more vulnerable populations. The Labour Market Framework has established a set of principles broadly accepted by key stakeholders and has mechanisms that allow for input into policy and planning. The Framework as it stands applies to the territorial level but there are opportunities to make it more sensitive to local conditions.

Local labour market networks could be established using the membership of the Framework Committees. These networks could be tasked with increasing the knowledge base on the unique conditions and challenges that exist at the local level in the Yukon and developing interventions and mechanisms that address those challenges. These networks could also contribute to stronger capacity building activities at the local level in the Yukon. For example, the networks could play an advisory role to the college in ensuring that courses are well aligned with local economic development opportunities as well as influencing the service delivery arrangements of employment services.

Yukon College has developed a First Nations Leadership Training (FNLT) programme in conjunction with Yukon First Nations that focuses on self-government. The First Nations leadership training is unique in its focus and is widely seen as an important part of building long-term success at the community level and ensuring the depth of leadership needed to govern all aspects of devolved responsibilities. Approaches which improve local governance capacities are welcomed and additional opportunities should be explored to encourage this type of activity.

Recommendation: Place a policy priority on increasing the engagement of employers with the vocational education system to ensure they are providing advice on the relevancy of programmes and curriculum

Mechanisms to increase the voice of employers in skills development opportunities remain underdeveloped in the Yukon. Efforts are being made through Yukon College which is developing an employer network to strengthen planning and performance management. Part of the challenge of developing stronger employer engagement mechanisms stem from the efforts of the College to respond to a broad series of priorities that include high public sector job demands for professional, technical and administrative personnel and an emergent need for leadership development among self-governing First Nations communities.

Yukon has a single postsecondary institution responsible for providing the very wide range of vocational educational courses associated with an expanding labour force. The college administration has been increasing the amount of contact with the local business community and acknowledges that more can be done. During this OECD review, business leaders noted that their voice remained weak and they are ready to participate in more efforts to align skills development opportunities with their needs.

Yukon College should ensure that the envisioned employer network plays a stronger advisory role in ensuring that programmes and curriculum are well aligned with local economic development opportunities. Yukon could look to Ontario, where programmes and courses delivered by each college are well informed by local demand. Each college has a Programme Advisory Committee, which reports to the President of the college through a Board of Governors. This Committee helps to define graduate requirements and course content (OECD, 2014a).

The College is also ideally positioned to work with the Yukon Government in workforce development strategies to increase employment opportunities. More efforts need to be place on upgrading the skills of already existing workers in the workplace. This can often be difficult as lower-skilled workers are typically less likely to participate in workplace training opportunities. The Yukon-Canada Job Grant will certainly offer an opportunity to provide more training opportunities in the workplace. Priority areas have been identified as Yukon Education has developed the Workfutures website which highlights the top 100 in-demand jobs. In the implementation of the programme, the government should ensure that training is also geared towards low-skilled individuals. The government should also consider how best to target workplace training opportunities to traditional low-skill sectors, such as retail and tourism.

Recommendation: Develop an entrepreneurship strategy, which focuses on youth and older workers and indigenous people as a tool for economic adjustment and job creation

Yukon has a culture of risk taking and self-sufficiency as well as an excellent track record of business creation. For both youth as well as older workers, entrepreneurship can support them to exit unemployment and generate economic value. OECD research has highlighted the importance of strong connections between vocational education and industry in promoting entrepreneurial activities. It is important that vocational education programmes stimulate entrepreneurial capacity and behaviour. This can be done by

Box 7.2. **Targeting the tourism sector in Blackpool, United Kingdom**

Tourism is central to the local economy in Blackpool, in the United Kingdom. Having long been a seaside resort that caters for high volume but low-spending customers, Blackpool is working hard to raise its game and attract higher spending customers through offering a higher quality tourism 'offer'. The town has been growing its branded attractions (e.g. Madame Tussauds, Nikolodean, Merlin) while also investing significantly in infrastructure (trams, cycles, buying the Blackpool tower for the public, new concert hall, refurbished front). It was recognised that capital and infrastructure investments alone will be insufficient to realising the town's vision, and that alongside them there is a need for investment in skills, particularly in the area of customer service. This meant investment in specific skills (for example through local college courses geared to the tourism industry) but also more informal learning and knowledge sharing.

A particular emphasis has been placed on informal skills development to raise the aspirations of service personnel so that they project a better image of the town and at the same time become more committed both to Blackpool, their employers and their own personal career prospects. A good example of such an initiative is the Welcome to Blackpool initiative which trains local people (especially those working in hospitality, leisure, tourism, transport and retail sectors, but also local residents) in appreciating the history of Blackpool, current developments and future plans. Through course attendance participants learn more about Blackpool's attractions and services. The knowledge gained can then be used to enhance visitor and local residents' experience of Blackpool.

Employers have reported that the short course equips staff to deliver a high standard of customer service, which in turn impresses visitors to the town and encourages word of mouth recommendations and repeat visits to Blackpool. The initiative has shown that taxi drivers, those involved in tourism, and local residents can be excellent ambassadors for Blackpool It was reported that over 3 000 people (of all ages) have attended the course in two years and that more than 250 organisations have benefited. Such initiatives have been useful in increasing staff retention in local firms, which traditionally have had high turnover rates, linked to the seasonality of tourism in the town. High turnover rates have been seen by some firms as representing a challenge in terms of investing in staff training and skills upgrading. Growing staff retention has allowed local employers such as the Sandcastle Water Park to start working with individuals on personal development plans.

Source: Froy, F., S. Giguère and M. Meghnagi (2012), "Skills for Competitiveness: A Synthesis Report", *OECD Local Economic and Employment Development (LEED) Working Papers*, No. 2012/09, OECD Publishing, Paris, *http://dx.doi.org/10.1787/5k98xwskmvr6-en*.

providing more opportunities for entrepreneurship in curricula, creating new guides and training for teachers, and developing new forms of assessment and accreditation.

Secondary school efforts can also focus on entrepreneurship education by using learning activities, which focus on active learning and real-life situations. Students should learn about business planning, accessing start up financing through the setting up of simulation or real businesses enterprises. Yukon College lists a course on "Introduction to Entrepreneurship", which is designed to assist students with determining what they need to build a successful private business. In addition to supporting students in their effort to expand upon their ideas and develop a roadmap for their business career, the course is also designed to provide mentorship opportunities to participants. It appears that the course is not currently offered and it is not clear whether the reason is lack of demand or other reasons. Yukon should undertake a review of existing initiatives with the goal of strengthening the system and ensuring a focus on the development of entrepreneurship skills.

The Yukon Chamber of Commerce has played an important role in supporting entrepreneurship and small businesses in Yukon; therefore it would be a key partner in these types of efforts. A recent development is the creation of a Yukon First Nations Chamber of Commerce (YFNCC) located in Whitehorse. The YFNCC provides a base for First Nations entrepreneurs and businesses to come together.

Recommendation: Develop a youth employment strategy focusing on pathways to success with the goal of reducing early school leaving, increasing participation in postsecondary education and connecting low-skilled youth to the labour market

Measuring youth unemployment in the Yukon is not easy. Small sample sizes mean that some statistics need to be suppressed especially where both gender and age cohorts are specified. Most recent reports indicate that the rate is around 6.9% which less than double the overall rate of which is 3.7%. Underreporting in First Nations communities likely mean the rates are higher. An examination of the 2011 National Household Survey indicates that non-response rate was above 25% for Yukon making this data source unreliable.

This observation appears to be supported by data from Yukon Education on secondary school graduation rates. For 2014 the graduation rate was 79% for non-First Nations but only 48% for First Nations. During this OECD review, employers reported that Yukon youth are not often employment ready, are prone to erratic work behaviour and that young people too often do not have sufficient work experience and employability skills. Too many youth have low aspirations and are frustrated by what they see as a lack of opportunity. Motivating young people can help them to recognise their personal and professional strengths, break out of old patterns of thinking and realise that they can attain their goals.

Yukon is unique in having a pre-school to college system that can act as an integrated whole for both non-First Nations and First Nations. Some of this work is already in progress. The federal and Yukon governments, Yukon First Nations, and the Council of Yukon First Nations have signed an MOU to support the educational success of First Nations students in the territory. The agreement will help launch a long-term strategic plan for First Nations student's life-long learning process focusing on the K-12 system. Yukon College also has a programme that targets early school leavers but more can be done and given the long term need of the Yukon to develop a skilled labour force, it is critical to ensure youth are supported in making labour market transitions. In many cases, youth require intensive and personalized support to build their ambition and motivation.

Mentorship programmes can have a positive impact; therefore Yukon should examine how to build stronger connections between youth and representatives from local employer groups and organisations. It is also important to establish stronger connections between local employers and high schools to make youth aware of the local job opportunities that are available and the expected educational pathways that need to be pursued for a job.

Recommendation: Establish a balance between employers needs for workers and job seekers needs for entry-level opportunities by instituting a requirement for a labour market assessment as part of the process of determining what skills will be sought through the Provincial Nominee Program.

The Labour Market framework has identified immigration as a key pillar signalling how important international migration is for labour supply. Yukon has been a welcoming place for newcomers and immigrants have made an important contribution to Yukon's economy and society. Yukon has run a successful Provincial Nominee Programme, which enables the territory to select internationally trained and experienced foreign workers who have the skills needed in the local labour market, and nominate them to receive Canadian permanent resident visas to settle and work in Yukon.

A number of local employers in Whitehorse and Dawson City rely on the Provincial Nominee Programme to fill their skills needs. Employers cite reliability, strong work ethic, and low turnover as significant advantages of individuals who participate in the Provincial Nominee Programme. During this OECD review, employment service providers and job seekers reported that the extensive use of the Provincial Nominee Programme has reduced the supply of entry-level jobs and employment opportunities.

Going forward, consideration should be given to instituting a requirement for a labour market assessment as part of the process of determining what skills will be sought through the Provincial Nominee Program. The Labour Market Framework committees bring many of the relevant stakeholders together and could be used as the mechanism for identifying and proposing changes to the Programme.

Yukon could also look to establish stronger public-private partnerships to providing more entry level positions. Employer Resource Networks in the United States have been successfully used to address similar problems and represent a demand driven employer-led approach to providing entry level positions while providing employers with support they need to manage an entry level workforce.

Box 7.3. **Employer Resource Networks in the United States**

ERNs grew out of two concurrent initiatives in 2000 local employers' need to reduce turnover among low-wage workers and a community consensus to reduce poverty. Issues that may catalyze an ERN model include: employee retention; presence of a skills gap between employer needs and employees' current skills level causing vacancies in higher paying middle skilled jobs; poverty reduction in the low-wage workforce; family financial literacy and asset development; and decreasing public assistance expenditures.

Primary stakeholders: ERN stakeholders include small to mid-sized companies and their employees; public human services and workforce development agencies; private non-profits; community colleges and vocational training organisations; and local, regional and national foundations and United Ways.

ERNs are consortia of businesses created to share the resources and expense of building the skills and capacities of their entry-level, often disadvantaged, workers.

Small and mid-sized businesses pool resources to accomplish together what they cannot accomplish individually – composed of several (e.g., 6-8) small and mid-sized businesses.

Services are targeted to entry-level workers but open to all employees – targeted to those most at risk for job turnover – low-wage, low-skilled, entry-level workers. All employees are able to access ERN services as needed, however. Participation in ERN services is voluntary for employees. Although, supervisors may include ERN services as part of a corrective action plan for workers with poor performance or behavioral problems that are disruptive to the work environment.

The primary focus is job retention, with a strong secondary focus on skill building – designed with the explicit goal of improving job retention of the existing workforce, and providing opportunities for skill building and advancement. Trainings may be industry-

Box 7.3. **Employer Resource Networks in the United States** *(cont.)*

specific or focus on general job skills training. ERNs also provide soft skills training on topics such as problem solving, time management, and conflict resolution.

Capacity is expanded through public and private partnerships – ERNs forge relationships with a mixture of local community partners – non-profits, public agencies, and community and technical colleges – to expand the range of resources they can make available to their employees. Where possible, ERNs rely on leveraged resources (funding and in-kind) from these partners or, because of the high volume of employees served or trained, pay for services from the community partner at a discounted cost.

ERNs provide a number of services to employers:

- Short-term, "high touch" case management – aim is to resolve any personal and family challenges that interfere with employment, such as: lack of transportation, childcare, or housing; relationship stress; mental health conditions; and drug or alcohol addictions. "Retention specialists" link employees with existing service providers in the community that offer different resources and services.
- Job and life skills training – create "shared-seat trainings" whose costs are shared by a number of businesses. Training may be: soft-skills training; job skills training (such as computer training); educational programmes (such as English as a second language and Spanish-language courses); and general trainings on asset development (financial literacy and home ownership).
- Specialised resources and supports – help improve employees' access to a range of work supports (e.g., preparation of income tax returns to ensure that eligible employees benefit from tax credits; wellness programmes with a focus on disease prevention and management, including health assessments, smoking cessation programmes, and fitness counselling).

The Success Coach from an ERN works with employees on-site at their place of employment before or after their work shift. ERN success coaches are not in central, social service locations but on-site at participating company workplaces. Their caseload is typically 1/3 that of a public case worker. Success coach accessibility and availability are keys to the ERN success: employees have immediate and direct access to counselling and referrals; and employers retain workers whose

References

Froy, F. and S. Giguère (2010), "Putting in Place Jobs that Last: A Guide to Rebuilding Quality Employment at Local Level", *OECD Local Economic and Employment Development (LEED) Working Papers*, No. 2010/13, OECD Publishing, Paris, *http://dx.doi.org/10.1787/5km7jf7qtk9p-en.*

Froy, F., S. Giguère and M. Meghnagi (2012), "Skills for Competitiveness: A Synthesis Report", *OECD Local Economic and Employment Development (LEED) Working Papers*, No. 2012/09, OECD Publishing, Paris, *http://dx.doi.org/10.1787/5k98xwskmvr6-en.*

Government of Yukon (2014), "On the Path Together: Wellness Plan for Yukon's Children and Family", Whitehorse, *www.yukonwellness.ca/pdf/wellnessplan.pdf.*

OECD (2014a), *Job Creation and Local Economic Development*, OECD Publishing, Paris, *http://dx.doi.org/10.1787/9789264215009-en.*

OECD (2014b), *Employment and Skills Strategies in Canada*, OECD Reviews on Local Job Creation, OECD Publishing, Paris, *http://dx.doi.org/10.1787/9789264209374-en.*

OECD (2014c), *Employment and Skills Strategies in the United States*, OECD Reviews on Local Job Creation, OECD Publishing, Paris, *http://dx.doi.org/10.1787/9789264209398-en.*

ORGANISATION FOR ECONOMIC CO-OPERATION AND DEVELOPMENT

The OECD is a unique forum where governments work together to address the economic, social and environmental challenges of globalisation. The OECD is also at the forefront of efforts to understand and to help governments respond to new developments and concerns, such as corporate governance, the information economy and the challenges of an ageing population. The Organisation provides a setting where governments can compare policy experiences, seek answers to common problems, identify good practice and work to co-ordinate domestic and international policies.

The OECD member countries are: Australia, Austria, Belgium, Canada, Chile, the Czech Republic, Denmark, Estonia, Finland, France, Germany, Greece, Hungary, Iceland, Ireland, Israel, Italy, Japan, Korea, Latvia, Luxembourg, Mexico, the Netherlands, New Zealand, Norway, Poland, Portugal, the Slovak Republic, Slovenia, Spain, Sweden, Switzerland, Turkey, the United Kingdom and the United States. The European Union takes part in the work of the OECD.

OECD Publishing disseminates widely the results of the Organisation's statistics gathering and research on economic, social and environmental issues, as well as the conventions, guidelines and standards agreed by its members.

LOCAL ECONOMIC AND EMPLOYMENT DEVELOPMENT (LEED)

The OECD Programme on Local Economic and Employment Development (LEED) has advised governments and communities since 1982 on how to respond to economic change and tackle complex problems in a fast-changing world. Its mission is to contribute to the creation of more and better quality jobs through more effective policy implementation, innovative practices, stronger capacities and integrated strategies at the local level. LEED draws on a comparative analysis of experience from the five continents in fostering economic growth, employment and inclusion. For more information on the LEED Programme, please visit *www.oecd.org/cfe/leed*.

OECD PUBLISHING, 2, rue André-Pascal, 75775 PARIS CEDEX 16
(84 2016 06 1 P) ISBN 978-92-64-25920-1 – 2016

www.ingramcontent.com/pod-product-compliance
Ingram Content Group UK Ltd.
Pitfield, Milton Keynes, MK11 3LW, UK
UKHW051505290926
15471UKWH00008B/1441

9 789264 259201